- THIS IS THE FIRST ISSUE OF -

Buckman Journal

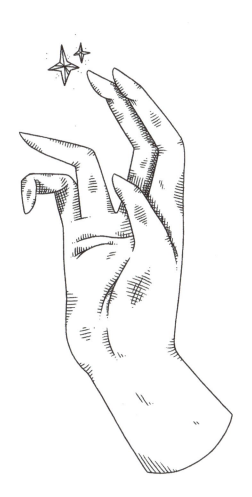

Portland, OR
Buckmanjournal.com
Buckman Publishing, LLC

THE BUCKMAN TEAM IS

Editor In Chief
the temp

**Managing Editor &
Creative Director**
Raechel Wolfe

Journal Designer
Jodie Beechem

Guidance Counselor
Eve Connell

ISBN: 978-1-7323910-0-0

CONTENTS

ARTWORK CONTRIBUTORS

Jodie Beechem

Jodie is an illustrator and designer living in Portland, OR. She is constantly inspired by scientific illustrations, art history, and anything remotely spooky. When she's not being creative, she's usually either watching live music at a local venue, or is at an arcade playing pinball.

www.jodiebeechem.com

Brendon Burton

Brendon Burton is an American visual artist based in Portland, Oregon. Brendon spent his childhood on a farm in an isolated community where he developed his distinct style and interest in vacant and decaying places. His work focuses on studying the side effects of cultural isolation and the concept of liminal space. Experienced in shooting fine art, documentary and fashion photography his work has been featured internationally in numerous galleries and publications.

www.brendonburton.com

Jamila Clarke

Jamila Clarke is a photographer living in the urban wilds that are the Pacific Northwest, its cities, forests and seaside providing a backdrop for her work. She discovered her first camera at eight and fell in love with film in middle school but it wasn't until she discovered digital photography that everything came together. She is able to create impossible moments, narratives worthy of folktales and add a little magic to everyday life.

www.jamilaclarke.com

Braeden Cox

Braeden Cox is an artist working and living in Portland, Oregon. Born in Eugene, Oregon she has also lived in Christchurch, New Zealand and Knoxville, Tennessee. She studied at the University of Oregon in Eugene where she earned a dual major in Fine Art and Digital Art. Braeden went on to complete her BFA degree in Digital Art at the University of Oregon's Portland campus. My digital collages, created through photographs and produced mainly in Photoshop, comment on the intersection of the man-made with the naturally occurring. The images present surreal landscapes that challenge reality.

www.braedencox.com

Stephanie Hatch

Stephanie Hatch is a mixed-media artist, currently working in Portland, OR. She has been exhibiting her work in Oregon and Northern California for 15 years. In 2006 Stephanie received her BA in Art from Southern Oregon University where she focused on painting, drawing, and black and white photography.

www.stephaniehatch.com

Annika Izora

Annika Hansteen-Izora (she/her/hers) is a queer, Black poet, artist, and activist. She believes in the power of Black joy, of protecting Black girl rage, and uplifting the stories and magic of the women before her.

www.instagram.com/izora.rises

M3AT

M3AT is the alias of Lorena Guerra Matteucci, a painter living in Vancouver, WA and participating in the art communities of Portland and Lake Oswego, OR and Vancouver, WA. She paints with acrylic and gouache on custom cut, treated, and framed wood panels.

www.m3at.bigcartel.com

Susan Sage

Susan Sage is a self taught portrait artist based out of Portland, OR. She has been experimenting in portraiture all her life and painting professionally for over a decade. Her acrylic portraits feature rich colors and locales containing friends playing dress up. Her paintings are based on reference photos from photoshoots in which she arranges and costumes her friends in elegant, old-fashioned approximations of what characters in museum paintings tend to look like. It is far from authentic. It is fun.

www.susansageart.com

Ruth Shively

Ruth Shively is a painter living in Portland, Oregon. She studied drawing and illustration in school but is a self taught painter. She loves the spontaneity of the paint and using color to create space. Going by instinct and immediate feelings about an image, she is drawn to stark positive/negative space, leaving the background simple, concentrating on the figure.

www.ruthshively.com

Kate Woodman

Born in Darmstadt, Germany, Kate Woodman was raised in Connecticut and currently calls Portland, Oregon home. A structural preservation engineer by training, Kate developed her love of photography in 2011 while investigating earthquake damage in New Zealand. Her engineering background serves her well, provoking a sense of balance and attention to detail in her photography and engendering an inventive approach to the technical challenges of creating an image. This, in conjunction with her love for all things classical, render her aesthetic clean and timeless—a nod to the past but assuredly modern in appeal.

www.katewoodman.com

Wooden Cyclops

Wooden Cyclops is the alias of Wesley James, an illustrator living in Portland, OR.

www.instagram.com/woodencyclops

LETTER FROM YOUR FRIEND, THE EDITOR

My name it is nothing,
my age it means less.
—Robert Zimmerman.

I'm one of those who nods a good-day to strangers while strolling through the neighborhood. There used to be more of us, but our numbers are thinning. The theory behind this act of polite acknowledgement is simple and basic. We want a friendly community, peaceable and kind; all the aspects that exemplify the better side of human nature. These qualities do not arise from standoffish aloofness, attention buried in a phone.

It's how I met the actor Steve Buscemi, back in the mid-2000s, right here in the Buckman neighborhood of Portland, Oregon. He was walking out of the original Hal's Tavern on SE Morrison, looking flummoxed, steps stuttering, right eye twitching. People often appeared in this state walking out of Hal's, especially new-comers.

"Good evening," I said with friendly smile.

"I just lost fifty bucks in shuffleboard against a geriatric," Buscemi replied.

I stopped, figuring my presence might offer condolence.

Buscemi continued. "He's been drinking for 15 hours. The guy can't pee straight, but he slides pucks as if he has a power over them, like they're his goddamn shaman stones or something. Jesus. One minute he was using his right hand then the next he's using his left. He's so old and drunk that he doesn't know if he's left or right handed."

"That's Dan Dobbek," I said. "He used to be a professional baseball player, major league. Was on the 1960 all-rookie team. Batted left, threw right."

"Somnabitch," said Buscemi. "I thought he was some sort of shuffleboard idiot savant."

"Well, that's how some graft. They come on pathetic."

"I should have seen it coming. I am ashamed of myself."

I asked, "What are you doing here, anyway. Some sort of Coen brothers movie?"

"No. Nothing like that. I have an uncle that lives here."

"I'm sorry you lost money," I said. "There's a small bar around the corner. Come on, I'll buy you a drink, Buscemi."

"I'll take you up on that but what are we, in the army? For chrissakes, call me Steve."

I took Steve to a dive bar that is no longer a dive bar. This was before the indoor smoking ban. Inside, layers of haze and condensated breath from brown lungs rose and fell like a polluted lava lamp, distorting the definition of people. Steve loved it. We rolled dice and he made some of that fifty back. The locals and bartender didn't mind losing to him. Steve was happy, their genial mood brought out his best qualities, and he cracked jokes, told epic tales of 1980's New York that entertained everyone well after closing time.

It was late, around 4am, when Steve eagerly accepted a challenge to wrestle Tad Chi, a carpenter who is half Korean, half Iowa redneck. Tad said Iowa concrete rassling was tough. Steve said that back in the day he was a ringolevio champ on the streets of Brooklyn, and there's no tougher wrestling than that. When I left, they were both on the floor in each other's head-locks, twisting to gain leverage. Steve's face was red, the tendons of his neck taut, and even though his teeth were grimacing, there was a devilish smile in it.

Yeah, Old Portland was great, but I don't expect it to remain. Life doesn't work like that. I may hold sentimentality for the past, only because I use it to craft the future. That's what the past is supposed to be for, all that 20-20 hindsight has got to beworth something.

BUCKMAN is an accumulation charging into the New Portland living room. Some will say moose on the loose. Others liken it to the dash and leap of gazelles. Whatever, the presence of BUCKMAN is a wild force disrupting the boring sameness infiltrating our society. Put down the phone, remove the standoffishness. Hello. Good day. Come on in, the neighborhood is fine.

the temp

THE HOT BOX

Words by Craig Foster
Artwork by Wooden Cyclops

Craig Foster is an editor based in Portland, Oregon who has stories and art published in *Box* and *The Newer York*, spouted commentary on a variety of perceived social missteps via an odd folio called *The Door Is A Jar*, and created the online architecture/design magazine *Peer*. These ventures no longer exist and he realizes the claims therefore beggar belief. Thankfully, he is not a proud man.

Every act on No-Talent Night at Al's Bar lives up to expectations.

This time it started with Paint Box, a twee duo from Fullerton who played Joy Division covers on ukulele and zither. They'd planned for three songs but got kicked after one and change, and apologized for any bother they might have caused.

It had been a scorcher and the bar offered no relief, even though by design it properly shut out the sun. No fans, no air conditioning, and the place reeked of leaky skin, dirty bedclothes, and sunscreen.

There was a large oilcloth stretched behind the stage from one end to the other. This read CATOLITICA CONVERTER in thick black strokes of a paintbrush, the Cs crossed out with Xs and a faint Perverter scrawled underneath in crayon. The large drum kit already in place suggested this was the night's one legit band waiting off-stage to play a proper set once the talentless were done.

After Paint Box got ousted, Rhythm Box (no relation) took the stage. No instruments. Just a grocery bag and three people dressed as lifeguards. One bikini and two trunks. The bikini would pull some product out of the bag and one of the trunks would apply it to the other trunk. Grape jelly, baked beans, yogurt. With each new item, the crowd—16 people, not bad—would belch admiring noises. A few started shouting out items they wanted to see get used. "Cajun seasoning!" "Molasses!" "Red dye #2!" The trunks, anticipating this, said in a stereo monotone, "We don't do requests."

A few started throwing their plastic beer cups at the lifeguard trio. Only one managed to connect, and the thrower shouted, "I want cheese! You can't leave without doing cheese!"

As if by some kind of crap magic, the last item produced was a tub of cream cheese. The good kind. The thrower screamed with delight. "You fuckers! You beautiful fuckers!" He tore off his t-shirt, threw it at a sulking Paint Box, and jumped onto the stage, grabbing his prize from the bikini. He struggled to break the seal, his hands being wet with beer and sweat, but finally managed and took deep fingerfuls of the white whip, smearing it in his armpits, across his chest, a little behind the ears, and some for a moustache. He raised his arms in victory and made for the trunks, as if to demolish them with a violently grateful hug. In their rush to escape, the trunks slipped on all the dripped foodstuffs and fell to the floor. The thrower, with outstretched arms and legs, dove on top.

Seeing this flying X land onto what most considered a highly successful talentless team, the audience stormed the stage and broke into a spasm of slides and spills.

From the wings, the lead singer of Catolitica Converter told the rest of the band that they couldn't and shouldn't go on.

It's good to know when it's not your night. ❿

> ## "I WANT CHEESE! YOU CAN'T LEAVE WITHOUT DOING CHEESE!"

Once there were two massage therapists who fell in love and had a child named Julia. She was a sweet, loving child who spoke with her hands just like her mother. When she placed her hands on someone's shoulder, instantly the person would relax. Her parents took this as a sign that their daughter's destiny lay in the field of massage therapy, and they started teaching her their secrets. But when Julia turned sixteen, she grew very ill and died.

The parents scattered Julia's ashes across the vegetable garden in their backyard, and in the center of the garden grew a pumpkin, large as a human head. No matter how many times the pumpkin was picked, a ripe one was in its place the next morning. This was how the parents knew Julia never completely left them. A year later another child was born and she, too, was named Julia because, for her parents, there was no other name.

New Julia turned out nothing like her sister. New Julia was very plain. Her dull, brown hair didn't shine red in the sun, and on the rare occasions when she did smile it was only a tiny smirk. She refused hugs, nor did she like to shake hands. She stopped bathing because she knew she would never be as clean as her dead sister. A stink hung over Julia like a swarm of bees and she wore her hair in one long, greasy braid down her back.

At school, she did chemistry labs by herself because no one wanted her as a partner. In gym, no one picked her for their team.

KISS FIGHT KISS
KISS FIGHT KISS

Words by Jessica Dylan Miele
Photography by Kate Woodman

Jessica Dylan Miele is a writer and librarian living in Portland, Oregon. Her short stories have been published in numerous literary magazines including *Coming Together*, *Quail Bell*, and *Gravel*. She was also featured on the *Short Stories Podcast*. You can find her online at JessicaReads.com.

An earlier version of Kiss Fight Kiss previously appeared in *Gingerbread House Literary Magazine*.

In her sophomore year, as she walked by a group of girls in blue and gold tracksuits, one of them yanked Julia's braid. Without thought, a pure reflex reaction, Julia turned around and slammed her fist into the girl's cheek. Squaring her shoulders, she tucked in her chin and prepared herself for the next blue and gold tracksuit but the girl standing closest screamed and ran. The others scrambled a retreat, too. Julia went home shaking with disappointment that the fight didn't continue. Frustrated, she allowed her mother to wrap a blanket around hershoulders and spoon-feed pumpkin soup.

AFTER THAT DAY, FIGHTING WAS ALL JULIA COULD THINK ABOUT.

Weighed with despair, she wandered inside a bird store and opened all the cages. The mass escape of birds was a flaming burst of squawking colors. The store was owned by a widow named Mary, small-footed with sharp elbows, usually a well-mannered woman but now enraged. Widow Mary charged screaming, her long fingernails clawing at Julia's small

"Try taking a hot bath," Julia's mother said but didn't press the issue.

After that day, fighting was all Julia could think about. But it proved difficult to find a fight. No one wanted to mess with someone so young and skinny, and especially because she was a girl. Nights she spent searching dubious streets, baring her teeth and shouting insults at drunks and addicts. But they laughed in her face.

face. At first, Julia crouched down low and was still, taking time to taste her own blood. Then she sprung upward and rammed into the widow with her shoulder, driving her across the room, smashing the old woman into the wall as one last green feathered flash escaped into the foggy outside.

Julia was arrested and sentenced to six months of community service at the Humane Society. Every morning there were several people in the parking lot, men, women, and teenagers, ready to avenge Widow Mary.

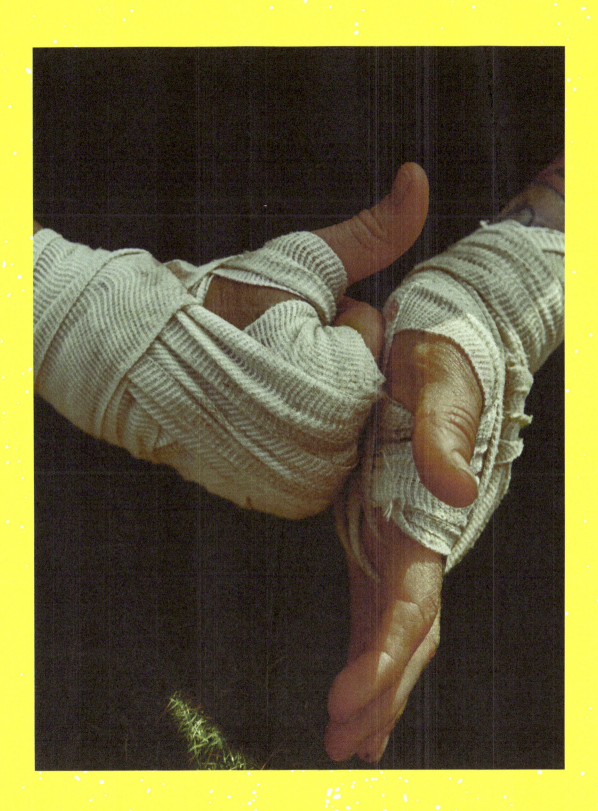

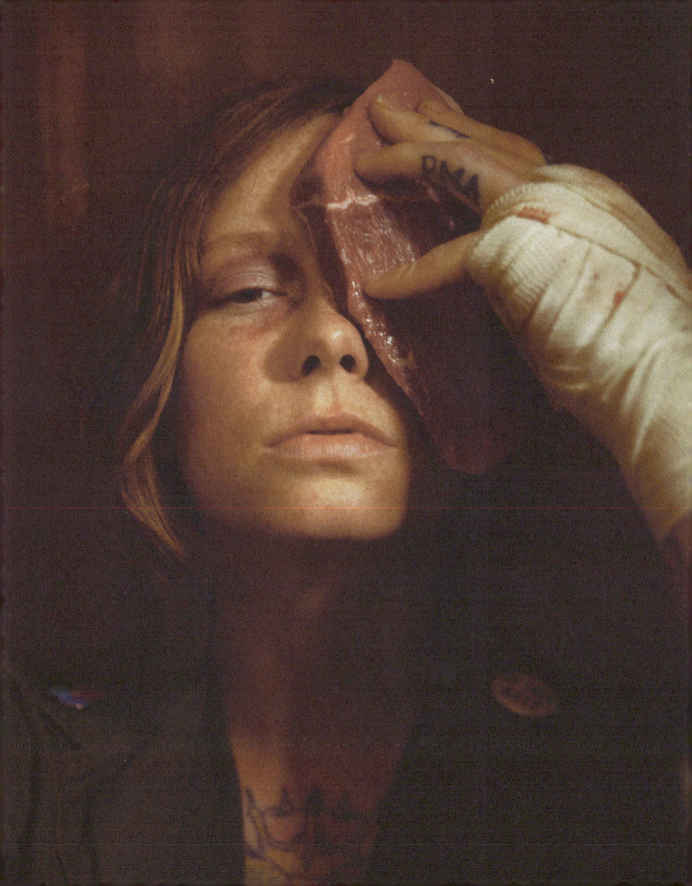

There was something about the way she fought that made Julia beautiful, even as she spat out a tooth. At first, people watched in disdain, but because Julia was so waifish and combated so recklessly, they soon cheered. She was swift and graceful, stunningly bold, and held nothing back as she flew at opponents with a frightening display of disregard for her personal safety. When she was struck, even with a most unmerciful blow, she was a shining beauty with fresh blood glossing across her face. She absorbed the pain with not even a moan, smiling ever so slightly as she turned her head and growled.

The crowds grew. She began to shower, the mix of the salve and wounds perfumed her presence, boys and men alike found it intoxicating, asked her for kisses, and sometimes she would oblige and other times she would lean in slowly and bite the hopeful's cheek. One boy with green eyes longing for a kiss was Henry, and though he stood in the very front of the crowd and cheered, he never dared to touch Julia.

Clumps of Julia's hair clogged the shower drain and her blood trailed the house, but Julia's parents made no mention. Once, while her mother was rubbing sirloin steaks with pepper, Julia snatched one that wasn't seasoned and smacked the raw meat onto her eye, leaning against the wall, sighing as she did so.

"That was your dinner," said her mother.

"I'll still eat it," said Julia. "I'm starving."

"I'm glad that you've found your appetite," said her mother.

"I'm not," said Julia's father, who entered the kitchen clacking his grilling tongs, surprising Julia. The cheeriness in his voice wavered, like a weak signal from a radio station. "When you don't eat, that's a second helping for me."

Julia lifted her chin, showing her bottom row of teeth. She looked at her father with her

DYING BECAME PART OF HER ACT

uncovered eye. "I'll fight you for it," she said. Her father was a large man but soft.

"What did you say, young lady?" asked her father, raising his tongs.

"Let it go," said her mother. "We will not acknowledge such behavior."

Sometimes Julia would fight three people in a day, one right after another, and the day she fought a fourth person was the day she died. She knew she was too tired to fight a fourth person, and she was on her period. But when someone new started coming at her with fists, she automatically tucked herself in and waited to leap and pounce. She was already having trouble standing on her left ankle, and tiny starbursts of light flickered at the edges of her vision.

"I came from very far away," her opponent said. His voice was high-pitched, and he had small hands. He punched her on her left side, and punched again, cracking a rib. Julia fell, the crowd encircled. Julia felt his shadow over her and it paused. The crowd was silent, not a breeze stirred. Then he kicked her in the forehead with the steel toe of his boot.

It was a good death. A light shot through Julia's mind and filled her body until she was nothing but a brightness co-mingling with her sister. Julia didn't know how she knew it was her sister enveloping her, but she accepted it wholeheartedly.

When she fell back into her body, a warmth kissed her mouth, and it filled her with an enthusiasm for life. Julia's vision came into focus. She saw a green-eyed boy, a streak of her blood across his lips. Julia smiled her tight smirk.

The son of two jewelry thieves, green-eyed Henry never thought he would amount to much. At seventeen, he already dropped out of high school. He mopped floors at the city art museum and tried not to look at the works of art, fearing he wouldn't comprehend them. He lived in a small apartment with a couple that made love loudly, and he spent his nights awake in the kitchen, contemplating spoons. He dated one girl, briefly, whose name also happened to be Julia, although he couldn't remember anything about her now that this Julia was in his arms.

That first night when he brought her back to his bedroom, she climbed on top of him and the bruises she wore like tattoos faded from purple to yellow to gone. Her crooked, broken nose readjusted itself to a delicate, smooth slope. "Am I really doing this to you?" Henry asked, his fingertips gently following the curve of her hips. "Am I really healing you? Me?"

"You," said Julia, and she bent forward, placed her mouth over his, breathing in his breath, the corners of her lips twitching.

Julia still didn't like to lose but now that she had Henry to save her, dying became part of her act. There was enough of a following to make a healthy amount of money from tips. Julia and Henry moved their show in front of the fountain at the center of town and, even in the rain, a crowd would gather.

Henry quit his job, taking on the role of manager. "Don't tell the crowds to tip you," Henry said. "That's my job. Don't fight Delmonico. He's a cheater and a liar and it won't be a fight anybody will want to watch."

"Get away from me," Julia said. "Just give me five seconds of peace. I can't get any sleep when you are around. Five seconds."

"You'll never get away from me," said Henry. "Even when you are old, and your bones are brittle, I'll still be by your side."

"My bones will never be brittle," said Julia.

"I won't be able to kiss away your old age," said Henry. "But I promise to kiss every one of your gray hairs before bed each night."

19

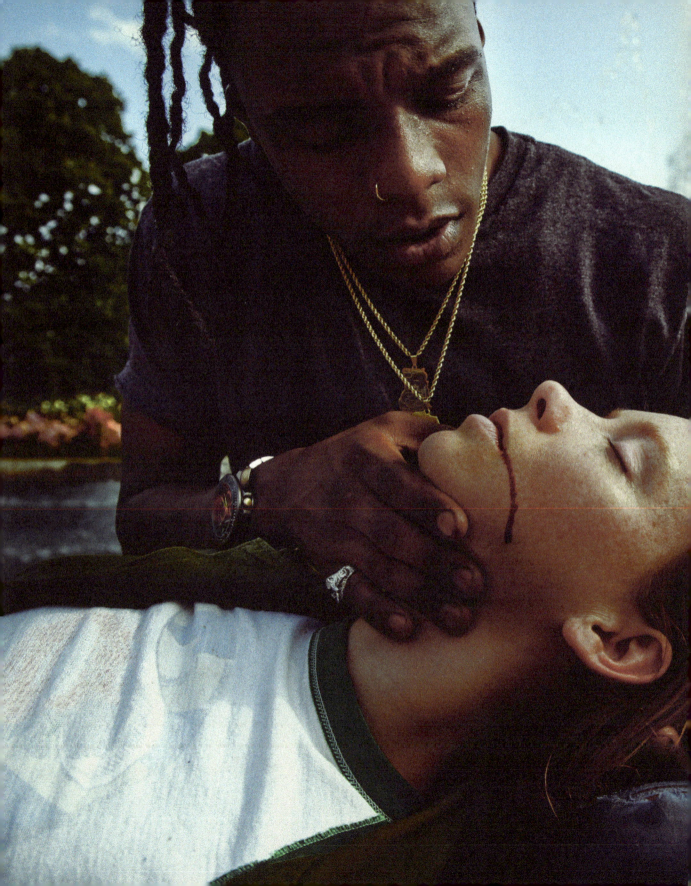

"I'm not gray yet," said Julia, giving Henry a hard shove, which only made him wrap his arms around her and squeeze her tightly, kissing her ear in the spot that would make her hear the echo of his kisses even in her sleep.

The fights became more elaborate. Henry rented fold-up chairs so people could sit down and eat their gravy fries while Julia was face-planted into the fountain steps. Cheers rose up even before the floppy-haired, green-eyed boy took center stage, cradling the unconscious Julia, brushing her hair away from her face as he met her lips.

"They enjoy watching me die," Julia said, touching a bloody spot on her forehead that refused to heal.

"Only because they are so sure that I'll come for you," said Henry. It was nighttime, and he was carrying a paper bag brimming with ripe peaches they bought from the Farmer's Market. He stepped in front of her and when he leaned in to kiss her forehead, the wound didn't close, but the bleeding ceased.

"They get disappointed when I win. It's not right."

Henry didn't respond. They were nearing Julia's parents' white clapboard house with a flickering porch light. In his arms, the peaches seemed to glow in the dark. "I don't see why you don't just move in with me," he said.

"Because," said Julia.

"Because."

"SHE THROWS AWAY HER LIFE EVERY OTHER DAY. SHE'S NO LONGER AFRAID OF DEATH. TELL ME, HOW IS SHE LIVING?"

"Because I need my sleep." She pinched him hard above his bony hip and caught a peach as it slipped from the paper bag.

He put down his bag of peaches to hug her, and he could feel the softness of the peach Julia held in her hand as it grazed the back of his neck.

"Please, let's go home," he said.

"I'll see you in the morning." She let him kiss her face once more before she went inside, and the porch light went out. Henry picked up his peaches and stared at the door as if he could see right through it, picturing Julia's hand pressed against the wall as she kicked a foot behind her to remove a sandal. When he guessed that she made her way upstairs to the bedroom, he moved around to the back of the house and sat down in the tender soil of the vegetable garden. He was eating his second peach when Julia's mother approached.

"You're ruining my sugar pea seedlings," Julia's mother said. "Please get up."

"Of course," said Henry. He shot to his feet, brushing the dirt off his pants. "Sorry, sorry. Would you like a peach?"

Julia's mother cocked her head to the side. In the dark, he couldn't make out the expression on her face. It was almost as if she had no face whatsoever. Julia's mother said, "Is that your dinner?"

"I suppose you could say that, yeah." Henry shrugged.

"Listen." Julia's mother's voice turned sharp. "You seem like a kind, young gentleman, but I must insist that you stay far, far away from my daughter."

Henry stepped closer to the older woman in hopes of seeing her face. How much of Julia was in this woman? "I can't do that," he said. "I'm the only one keeping your daughter alive."

"She throws away her life every other day. She's no longer afraid of death. Tell me, how is she living?" Julia's mother also advanced forward, holding an arm out and pointing a finger at his chest. "Without you, she would be able to get past all this fighting. She would be able to grow up and do something good for this world."

"If it wasn't for me, another daughter of yours would be ashes," said Henry. He pushed her finger away. With her other hand, Julia's mother very neatly put the boy to sleep by pressing her thumb into his neck. Laying him on the grass, she went into her kitchen to retrieve her set of knives and then she chopped Henry into tiny pieces. The whole night she spent making meals out of Henry's body and the golden peaches. She used up every bit she could and buried Henry's toenails, fingernails, hair, and other inedible parts around the pumpkin patch.

In the morning, Julia's father couldn't get over the glorious aroma from the kitchen. He ate as much as he could and packed more into Tupperware containers for lunch. "My wife loves me so much," Julia's father bragged to his clients at work. "Her cooking proves it to be so."

Julia couldn't get out bed because she was in too much pain. Even turning her head induced a jarring ring through her body. Blood was all over her pillow and sheets. Her nose was bent, her mouth wounded, and some teeth were missing. A rib poked out of her back. Eyes swollen. When her mother entered the bedroom, Julia could barely hear her mother's screams. An ambulance rushed Julia to the hospital. All she asked for was Henry. Instead they gave her morphine.

"Now you can stop fighting," her mother whispered into her ear. "And start doing something good for your body."

"There is no such thing," said Julia, her eyes trained on the hospital's white ceiling. A trickle of blood dribbled down the corner of her mouth.

"You are so young! Think of all the wonderful things you have to look forward to. All the places you could travel, all the things you could learn, the people you could meet."

"Henry," said Julia.

"That's enough of that now," said Julia's mother. "Henry is gone, and he is never coming back. You'll have to start seeing this as a good thing and let yourself be free. Don't throw your life away for a boy that has done nothing for you but disappear."

"He has not disappeared," said Julia. She wiped her mouth with the back of her hand. "He wouldn't do that. Not Henry."

"He has," said Julia's mother.

"Then he will reappear," said Julia.

The pumpkin in the vegetable garden grew fatter than ever, and then it began to weep. Saltwater rose from the earth, killing surrounding plants until only the pumpkin retained its color. Dead cats and squirrels accumulated around the patch.

As soon as Julia left the hospital, she dragged her body towards the fountain in the center of town. She was gone for so long that there were very few people wanting to see a show. A young couple held each other close and hurried away as bruised and pounded Julia made it known she had come for a fight. Swaying on her feet, eleventh rib re-poking out her back, Julia tucked in her chin and stationed her legs in fighter's stance. The only person that approached was Delmonico, bald and pale.

"Joyous day." Delmonico lifted half of his mouth into a smile. "We are at last to fight, am I not mistaken?"

"You are not," said Julia. She pushed out a breath of air to keep herself from gritting her teeth. Her tongue was dry and yet her mouth still tasted of blood.

"This will be the fastest fight you'll ever experience," said Delmonico. "Most painful, too." From his flannel jacket, the hairless man pulled out a long rope and lassoed it around Julia's neck, dragging her to the ground. There was no one to save her, no one even thought to help as the few watching waited for the girl to stop breathing so that the hero could swoop in and give them something to clap about. It took a long time for Julia to stop breathing. She lost several of her fingernails as she struggled to wrench free from the wet noose, kicking her legs, staring into the pale eyes of Delmonico. Eyes that had no lashes.

The pumpkin was trying to get a hold of Henry. It was trying to get Henry to go back for Julia, because she needed saving once more.

"It can't be me," Henry was saying. He was saying this over and over.

"It has to be you," the pumpkin was saying. "Your kisses are nothing like mine."

"But I've been eaten. I can't ever be the me I once was."

"It has to be you," the pumpkin was saying. "It has to be you."

Julia's mother came into the vegetable patch to collect the fattest pumpkin she had ever seen. She pulled out her butcher knife to cut off the orange top, the very knife she had used to cut off Henry's head.

"The pumpkin looks sick," said Julia's father. "Maybe we shouldn't eat this one."

"The pumpkin looks as it always has," said Julia's mother. "It's just bigger. I need to make a pie. I'm going to make a pie so delicious our daughter will forget any boy she has ever kissed, and every person she has ever fought." Swiftly, as she had been doing for years, Julia's mother stabbed her knife into the pumpkin. Lifting off the top, she dipped her hands to scoop out the seeds, but instead of seeds all she felt was something feathered. A green parakeet flew out, banging into the closed kitchen window again and again until Julia's father opened the window and out it soared.

At the fountain, Julia had died. 911 was called. Bowing over Julia was Delmonico, his bald face cloaked in tears and snot as he kissed her face and kissed her neck and kissed her lifeless hands. The rope was abandoned in the fountain.

The green parakeet dived from the sky, landed, and placed its beak on Julia's lips. It fluttered over the dark red burn marks on her neck. Delmonico reached up a hand to whap the bird away, but Julia lifted her head and said in a strong, clear voice, "Don't."

A lone woman clapped ecstatically.

Julia's mother and father were eating the last of Henry's heart in the kitchen when Julia entered the room, with the green parakeet perched on her shoulder.

"I'm going away," said Julia. "You have finally gotten your wish."

"I want you to travel," said Julia's mother. "But I certainly want you to come back. Where are you going? Are you going alone?"

Julia gave no answers. She glared at her mother, as did the parakeet.

"Oh," said Julia's mother, and it came out as a moan. She sank to her knees, crawling over to her daughter to kiss her beautiful, perfect hands, praying for the day that her daughter's hands would be too old to fold into fists. ◐

"YOUR KISSES ARE NOTHING LIKE MINE."

27

OLD PORT— LAND

Words by Rich Perin
Artwork by Jodie Beechem

Rich Perin was born and raised in Australia, but in the 1990s he escaped to the U.S.A. and has been on the run ever since. After several years based in Austin and San Antonio, Texas, he is currently holed-up in Portland, Oregon. His writing has appeared in *Adbusters*, *Harpur Palate*, *Bluestem*, and other publications.

n out of town family looks at the café from the sidewalk. The father is working towards pot-bellied. Growing jowls. A Ring of Saturn remainder of hair orbiting his mass of baldness. Polo shirt tucked into his belted shorts. Loafers. White socks. The mother's a fusser. She could enjoy the vivid sunflower-print dress she's wearing,but instead she's buzzing over her seven-year-old son, telling him to stop fidgeting, moving the fringe of his blonde hair away from his eyes. His older sister, a recent teenager, stands aloof, waits with headphones plugging her ears. The father approves the café and leads his family to its door.

As he's about to open the door, a bearded man in his twenties, wearing only boxer-briefs and a headband, triumphantly exits the café with a bulldog, a labradoodle, and a dachshund each reined to a master leash. The young man nods a good-day, salutes his coffee to the family, then walks away with his pack. The son points and a goofy, giant grin beams from his face. The mother slaps the boy's hand, but instead of pain he laughs and gestures that he wants to take his pants off. The teenage daughter is trying to take a photo of the dog-walker with her phone. The father moves his brood in the opposite direction, away from the café, to the food carts suggested by travel guidebook.

Eryn and Jasper watch from inside the café, standing behind the espresso machine. "Oh, don't go!" says Eryn. "I would have made the kids an awesome smoothie."

"I guess nothin'-but-underwear scares some," reasons Jasper.

"But he's walking around happy with three dogs who obviously adore him. That's not scary."

"It's weird, though."

"It's more sweet than weird. I like our regulars. They keep things interesting."

Jasper nods his head. "I'm with you. The half-dressed dog-walker always brings a smile to my face."

"Right?" affirms Eryn. "And what about Stavros. He's another that makes me smile."

Jasper prepares a fresh urn of drip coffee. "What is Stavros' story?"

"I think he has done a lot. Or at least seen a lot."

"But where's he from? The Philippines? Morocco?"

"I don't know," she responds. "I always thought he's from Mexico, but that's just an assumption."

"And what does he do? He's always got cash in his wallet. It makes me think that he's a gambler or a loan shark."

Eryn shakes her head and furrows her eyes. "It's nothing glamorous like that. He's a landlord."

But Jasper pursues the line of thought. "And he drives around that old Cadillac. Have you seen how long that thing is? I think the landlord is a front.

He might be a pimp!" He laughs at his assumptions.

"Whatever," says Eryn. "He's interesting. I closed Sunday and he kept me company. He told a story about his last visit to New York and hooking up with an ice-skater who had a third nipple."

"Wow," says Jasper. "Yeah, I bet he has no problems with the ladies."

Eryn moves to the food prep area. "No, it wasn't crass. There was more to it. Much more. He sets scenes, goes into details, delivers it with humor. You know how slow closing can be. It's fun when he hangs out and decides to chat. It beats leaning against the espresso machine looking at the clock."

"I wish he'd kick it with me," admits Jasper. "I'd really like to hear a kink story about three nipples. I should try to strike up a conversation with him. Maybe about music. Hey, do you mind if I put my tunes on?"

Blondie is playing in the background. "Sure," says Eryn. "But that means you have to make the food orders."

Jasper unplugs Eryn's phone and connects his to the house stereo. A contemporary RnB song with wandering female vocals, auto-tuned, and a heavy bass drum floods

"SO, WHAT'S THE STORY ABOUT THE THIRD NIPPLE?"

the speakers. "This is DJ Klue's remix of Beyoncé," announces Jasper with a raised voice. "Man, that beat has got some serious backbone!" Jasper sings along a few bars in falsetto, neck-snaps back and forth to the rhythm.

Eryn retrieves her phone and lowers Jasper's volume a little. He doesn't notice the lowered volume but soon notices Eryn is no longer talking. She is staring blankly towards the door. "So, what's the story about the third nipple?" asks Jasper.

Eryn turns to him. "There's no way I can recount it as good as Stavros. I'm not as funny. You should ask him to tell you."

Jasper considers. "Ha! That's weird. I mean, you know, giving him change for his coffee and then casually dropping, 'Hey, Eryn says you should tell me the story about the gal with the extra nipple.'"

Eryn smirks. "Sure, you should do it just like that. You're going to need a good ten minutes of free time, though. It's a story that shouldn't be rushed."

The café doors open. A mechanic from the auto repair store a block away enters and nods at Jasper.

BUCKMAN
NEIGHBORHOOD

WILLAMETTE RIVER

SE SANDY

SE MLK

SE GRAND

SE 7TH

SE 11TH

SE 12TH

"Hi," says Jasper. "How are you?"

"Alright," says the mechanic. "I'll just get a large coffee to go."

"That's three dollars."

As the mechanic leaves with coffee in hand, Jasper continues. "What is the lead-up to a three-nipple story, anyway?""We were talking about getting old, how the body and mind slip. Then Stavros says, 'Suicide is never off the table, Eryn.' I mean, wow, who says things like that?"

"Whoa! He's suicidal?"

"No, he says he's not. It's just an option always available. Anyways, I quoted a line by Spinoza that has always stuck with me." Eryn pauses and searches for the words. "A free man thinks of nothing less than of death and his wisdom is a meditation not on death but on life. I repeated that line when Stavros mentioned suicide. He smiled, thought about it, then recounted the New York story with the ice skater."

Jasper rakes his scrappy beard. "That sounds like a wild tangent."

"More like a nice tangent. It was his way of telling me that he gets what Spinoza is talking about."

"Cool, cool," says Jasper. "Has Lewis met him? Sounds like they would get along."

"No, not yet. He'll probably meet Lewis when he picks me up for the date."

Jasper freezes. "Date? Say what now?"

A carpenter enters the café, wearing overalls, a flat pencil behind his ear, a steel ring pierced through his nose, a silver-capped front tooth, salt-and-pepper billy-goat beard running down to his Adam's Apple, and around his neck a wooden rosary. He approaches the counter.

"Hi, Tad," says Eryn. "Just the coffee?"

"Ahoy hoy," replies Tad, and he places down a dollar seventy-five in quarters. "How you?"

"Good."

"Did you see what's hangin' from the power lines out front?" asks Tad.

"A pair of shoes?"

"No."

"I give up. What?"

Tad pumps coffee from the self-serve urn into his cup. He smiles wide, his silver-capped tooth glints. "You need to go and look yourself. It's something to be experienced, not spoken. Trust me not!" And with that, he exits through the back door to the patio smoking section.

Eryn and Jasper go outside and hanging from the power lines are a pair of dildos, flesh-colored, tied together with a shoelace. Like nunchucks. Eryn and Jasper turn to each other, laugh, and re-enter the café.

HE'S PICKING ME UP IN HIS OLD CADILLAC AND TAKING ME TO A FANCY RESTAURANT THAT HAS VALET PARKING. HOW OFTEN DOES THAT HAPPEN TO YOU?"

"HOLY SHIT!" EXCLAIMS JASPER.

"Dicks in the sky," jokes Eryn. "Dongs on a wire!"

Jasper joins in. "Dildo tight-rope!"

"I wonder if it is the result of a break-up?" queries Eryn with a mischievous smile. "Like, the ex stole the dildos and lobbed them up for everyone to see."

"Let that be a lesson," proclaims Jasper. "Hide your sex toys before breaking up."

Two people enter and order bagels. Then another arrives and orders a tuna melt. Jasper makes them faster than usual, then, while nonchalantly cleaning the counter, he asks, "So, you and Lewis are having problems?"

Eryn flatly answers. "Uh, no."

"Oh...." Jasper furrows his eyebrows, rubs the countertop with more elbow grease as if a beet stain is sinking deeper.

"I like Stavros but it's not like that," says Eryn. "He's really interesting. He's picking me up in his old Cadillac and taking me to a fancy restaurant that has valet parking. How often does that happen to you?"

"It's really none of my business," says Jasper, and he looks at other places that need a wipe.

"No, it's cool, you're not prying." She acknowledges, "I'm the one that brought up the subject."

Jasper throws the wipe rag into the laundry hamper and props himself against the fridge. "Wow...And Lewis knows?"

"Of course he knows!"

"Wow. Sorry, I mean...."

Eryn laughs.

Jasper blushes, but then he laughs, too. "I'm sorry," he says. Then, "You know, I'm just picturing Stavros knocking on the door of your house, dressed in a suit, with flowers. Here's a guy that might be old enough to be your dad, and he's going to meet the man of the house, your boyfriend, before taking you out on a date. That's a mixed-up role reversal."

"Ha!" Eryn exclaims with a smile and nod. "Yeah, that's not common. I don't think I am leading Stavros on. I hope not." She peers outside, looks for distance. "No, I'm not. He invited Lewis as well, but I said that's cool, we're just going out as friends. He needs friends, I think. He's lonely."

Jasper nods. "I wonder how old is he, anyway?"

"THAT'S A TOMATO."

"I don't know," says Eryn. "He was joking about killing himself when he turns 50."

"So, he's younger than 50. Maybe close?" queries Jasper.

"He's probably 56," answers Eryn.

They both laugh.

"You're right, though," Jasper admits. "I'd go to dinner with him if he asked me. A steak dinner."

Eryn looks at the clock. "I'm going to take lunch now if that's cool."

Jasper surveys the tables, the only people inside are two activists nursing coffees. "Sure. Whatcha having? I'll make it for you."

"That's sweet. But I'm just going to grab a bagel."

"How about a little bacon, sliced tomato..."

"No, I got my own tomato," and from her bag Eryn fishes out a large heirloom variety.

"Holy shit!" exclaims Jasper. "That's a tomato."

"Yes. Yes it is," says Eryn in deadpan. She then fumbles around in her bag and finds another. "Here, you can have this. I grew it myself."

"You grew it?"

"Yes." Eryn looks at Jasper with a serious face. "I am the Tomato Bandit of North Portland."

A July night, five years ago, Eryn and Lewis moved a futon to the front porch to claim the cool evening breeze. They were both listening to the crickets chirp when they heard a rustle in their front yard. It was their neighbor from across the street, an old lady with crooked back, on her knees digging. They quietly watched, unnoticed, as the old lady planted two tomato seedlings. After finishing their yard, she shuffled to the next and planted again. She embedded the entire block before returning home. Her house was a small cottage, with a worn dandelion pocked lawn, and rows of container plants where tin cans, buckets, and a pedestal sink were re-purposed into pots.

Most of the old lady's guerrilla tomatoes didn't last. One or two maintained, if in reach of automatic sprinklers. Eryn and Lewis watered and feed theirs, nurturing them to large vines bearing fat fruit. The old lady noticed. Every time she saw either Eryn or Lewis, she waved and smiled with a little laugh of joy. The old lady maintained her replant enterprise the next two years. But one winter, she was

stretchered to an ambulance. Her house was sold, demolished, and replaced with a three-story whose footprint claimed most of the property, leaving room only for a small flower-bed and thin strip of fresh lawn. That summer, though, tomatoes reappeared in the neighborhood with vengeance, not only on the block but in the surrounding blocks, including a thriving Roma next to the convenience store. In the small flower-bed across the street, the new homeowners discovered a young heirloom and watered the plant, which rewarded them with tomatoes the size of fists. The following year, the homeowners replaced the lawn with a planter box and grew more, as well as pole beans and kale.●

MOST OF THE OLD LADY'S GUERRILLA TOMATOES DIDN'T LAST.

THAT SUMMER,
THOUGH, TOMATOES
REAPPEARED IN THE
NEIGHBORHOOD
WITH VENGEANCE
THAT SUMMER,
THOUGH, TOMATOE
REAPPEARED IN TH

REALLY —————— AWESOME

Words by Tammy Melody Gomez
Paintings by Ruth Shively

Tammy Melody Gomez is an activist, performance artist, and writer whose work is published in collections including *Entre Guadalupe y Malinche: Tejanas in Literature and Art* (UT Press, 2016), and *Women in Nature* (Louise Grace Publishing, 2014). She is profiled in *Las Tejanas: 300 Years of History* (UT Press, 2003), and was honored by Goucher College (Maryland) with the "Alumnae/i Award for Excellence in Public Service" in 2010. As a 2015-2018 Black Earth Institute Fellow, Tammy guest edited the "Rewilding" issue of *About Place Journal* (May 2018). She is a proud member of the Macondo Writers Workshop.

Really Awesome And Poor first appeared in *BIKEQUITY: Money, Class, & Bicycling*, edited by Elly Blue and printed by Microcosm Publishing in Portland, Oregon (ISBN 978-1-62106-090-1).

 POOR —————— AND

It's just about that time. I can still make it if I hurry. Put on the layers of necessary jackets and scarves, and the helmet and lights that are mandated by the organizers and local bicycling laws.

But I probably won't go. Again. I'll stay away as I usually do, in a steady and now predictable pattern of letting go of excitement about bicycling.

Lest there be any doubt about it, I am a woman who loves to bicycle in her city and who, in fact, has been bicycling almost daily as an urban commuter who hasn't owned a car since about 2008. Which is saying a lot being from and residing in Texas. But I just can't get psyched anymore about joining social rides—the Sunday night, the Wednesday night, the regularly-scheduled group excursions-as I first did long ago.

It took some time for Fort Worth to warm to the idea of urban cyclists taking up precious lane space on the public streets. Taking anything away from cars and their operators is almost a sacrilegious act in this state. But now that the wheels of time are spinning in a new and progressive direction, the group and social rides and Facebook bike group pages are sprouting up here, too.

Unfortunately, the leaders and coordinators of the social rides tend to be of a specific and very limited demographic. I'll give you one guess. They decide for all of us where we will ride, selecting routes that bypass the neighborhoods or sections of town where my mother resides in the humble but well-built home I grew up in, where my 7-year old nephew gets his pan dulce and sometimes walks to school, and where my brother waits to catch the bus to get his dialysis treatments.

Most social riders might call these parts of town "dangerous," not realizing they're talking about areas I occupy, traverse, and pedal into—often by myself. They seem to have a locked-in rejection of or a lack of curiosity about what is not known, leading to an unwillingness to go and explore where they have never been before.

What ends up happening is that the social rides are mind-numbingly predictable and there seems to be no "edge" for possible growth and new discovery. We stop at the same pubs, ride down the same well-paved, gentrified streets and 'hoods. We are racing to a destination called sameness and that is a pablum that has no taste for me. Without flavor on the ride, I am reminded that mainstreamers are comfy with what they know. Hipster brewpubs, well-lit cupcake boutiques, bougie wine bars. But that's not me. I mean, I do enjoy beer, cupcakes, and, yeah, I'll take a glass of wine—but that's not the totality of me, nor my experience of this city.

Making the social rides about spending money along the way is another complication, particularly for those of us on a fixed-income or who live from paycheck to paycheck. It's not fun getting outed as a broke bicyclist when you're on social rides where folks are dropping twelve bucks on a cheese tray to go with their expensive artisanal pints. You kinda just want to stay home with your 40oz.

One late afternoon, back around 2008, I got dolled up and wrapped a gift before jumping into my slow-moving 1990's model Buick. I was a bit reluctant to drive, given that I hadn't paid my insurance premium for the month—saving that money for a greater need, I guess—but I did it anyway because of the friend whose birthday dinner was now in session. I just couldn't flake on her.

Long story short, I got pulled over and ticketed, and my instincts to stay home that evening totally finger-waved me for the rest of the week. Driving without insurance is a pretty serious offense and I faced a hefty fine. Years later, I look back and see that having my

WHEN YOU'RE A KID, YOU BICYCLE. AS AN ADULT, YOU'RE SUPPOSED TO OWN A CAR AND DRIVE IT TO THE GYM.

driving privilege temporarily suspended was actually a good thing for me. Not to mention that the Buick was in deterioration mode, with repair bills staring me down on an almost monthly basis. Finally, I just got fed up. I did the math and calculated that if I just let go of driving—for good—I could free up at least a hundred bucks per month to do things like buy more healthy food, see a movie every once in a while, and not have to fret about constant car problems jacking my checking account.

Beyond the financial savings, I've also had a strong commitment to sustainability. The prerequisite that my workplace be located close to where I live is paramount as I decide on choices for employment. My ethic is that I need to be able to, in a pinch, walk or bicycle to my workplace from home. On my knobby-tired mountain bike, I can pedal to work through woodsy Trinity Park—which has a pretty awesome hike-and-bike trail—in less than 25 minutes. That same distance can be walked (I've done it several times)

in about an hour. I love knowing that I am capable of doing this, and don't need to spend money relying on either a personal vehicle or even the limited mass transportation system in my city. I'm good to go with my own two feet and two wheels.

When people comment on how impressed they are that I bicycle everywhere I need to go, I tell them that my bike is my fitness center because I cannot afford to pay to work out at one of those places. They smile and nod, often adding that they wish they had the gumption to do as I do. It's not a brag, it's just the truth: I am too poor to spend money on things that, in an industrialized capitalist society, signify success and maturity. When you're a kid, you bicycle. As an adult, you're supposed to own a car and drive it to the gym.

shade of light brown—a color I associate with the Dust Bowl and the hardscrabble life of Americans during the Depression. But these kids didn't have a care in the world, or so it seemed, and the cleanliness of their clothing was the least of their worries.

I think of them sometimes as I bike to the store or to meet a friend at the museum on free day, wearing my non-technical bicycle gear, which in the wintertime often consists of leggings AND sweatpants and three to four layers of top wear: a t-shirt, a wool or cashmere sweater (thrift store, baby), a light jacket, and maybe the faux-down zippered coat. Pedaling along, I am often the most puffed up bicyclist on the trails

I WANT BICYCLING IN THE CITY TO LOOK ACHIEVABLE

There were some kids on my block, growing up in south Fort Worth, who seemed to be free-ranging wild children. I think I saw their mother maybe once or twice, but these kids were forever on the street, pedaling their two-wheelers farther away from their house than I was permitted to do. When they came to my end of the street, we circled each other for hours on end and I felt a little whiff of their freedom. They also had the dingiest underwear I'd ever seen, which fascinated me enormously. I couldn't imagine being out on the public streets showing my skivvies that

or streets, resembling the bulky bag lady who wears all the clothing she owns. It's not a pretty sight, but I simply don't want to buy the high-end technical bike garments and accessory gear that are manufactured and marketed for our consumption.

As a bicyclist in 21st century America, I don't care to be corralled into believing that I have to spend lots of money to dress the part of an urban cyclist. I will suit myself, even as it pains me to have to use a backpack to carry any utilitarian necessities (scarves, balaclava, sweater layers) when it becomes too warm to wear them all. I want bicycling in the city to look achievable—get a bike and you're there. You don't have to have the fancy crotch-padded Lycra shorts and hundred dollar handlebar lights. I also don't crave the comments that I sometimes get from cyclists with a bigger bank than me. I can tell the intentions are good, it's just in the saying that I am put off.

After a social ride, a guy once commented on my ratty, ripped bicycle seat. I had slipped a black balaclava over it, which was my poor people way of both covering the torn seat and adding more cushioning. He asked why I didn't just buy another saddle? They're only about twenty bucks.

AFTER A SOCIAL RIDE, A GUY ONCE COMMENTED ON MY RATTY, RIPPED BICYCLE SEAT.

Only. About. It's these two words that hit me hard every time. It's become a loud, resonating indictment uttered by the privileged to the poor: Money is plentiful and purchasing power is the solution to all problems. Ugh. It's quite shaming and reveals the absurd assumption that everyone bicycling on your social ride has the same financial capacity as you—or else should surely be trying their damnedest to attain it.

I do make pledges and promises to myself, on the level of money and how I choose to use it, at least once a week. If I just bundle up warmly and pedal on through the ice or mud, I'll reward myself with a coffee from Java Lab—for not having spent that cash on bus fare to get to work. Or sometimes I pep talk myself, saying, if you bicycle instead of taking a taxi, you can buy yourself a breakfast burrito and a coffee. It's a motivational tool for me to get my ass out of bed, onto the bike saddle, and to my destination on my own steam. Ultimately, it is exhilarating to arrive at my workplace, by 6:30 am, when it's 28 degrees outside—with the proverbial carrot that had dangled before me now transmuted into a small (but adequate for me) cup of fresh-brewed bistro coffee. This makes my sweaty back, aching calf muscles, and the poor state of personal wealth all worth the conscious effort. I'm toning my body while also adjusting my requirements for quality of life and happiness to a scale that is right for me.

I am an artist and practitioner of permaculture principles, which means that I have let go of many belief systems that don't work for me anymore. I also decided long ago that I want to live off "voluntary simplicity," which to the uninitiated sounds like I'm saying I want to be poor. Well, voluntary simplicity, on its face, does look like poor. It looks like needy, it looks like barebones living. And to some extent, it is. Practicing voluntary simplicity means I've unsubscribed from blind consumerism and adherence to precepts such as "the more you have, the wealthier you are" or "you can't be in the game if you don't look the part."

I'VE BEEN GIVEN A LICENSE TO BE DIFFERENT, TO NOT BE TYPICAL, WHICH ALLOWS ME THE FREEDOM TO GO AHEAD AND LIVE A REBEL EXISTENCE.

I'm a Latina in her early 50's who grew up on Neil Young and Neil Diamond, raised by bilingual U.S.-born parents. I haven't truly "looked the part" of a typical mainstream U.S. citizen since I was born. I'm a bonafide outsider according to the politics and social programming of many citizens that surround me. In a sense, I've been given a license to be different, to not be typical, which allows me the freedom to go ahead and live a rebel existence. And I am good with that because it means that normalizing expectations and restrictive social mores are mine to fuck with—to adapt for my personally-customized palette of aspirations, benchmarks, and measures of success and satisfaction.

I also kind of wish I could find those beige undies kids from my old neighborhood, who grew up white and poor and, hopefully, have made something really awesome of their adult lives. If they were to remember me, even vaguely, maybe they would join me in conversation about those early bike rides together—in the "dangerous" part of town—where we would tear down the streets, unfettered and unconcerned about how we looked as we pedaled towards a horizon of utter joy.🅑

HUMAN ACHIEVEMENT: PARTY

Words by Lauren Hunter
Artwork by Annika Izora

Lauren Hunter is the author of *HUMAN ACHIEVEMENTS* (Birds, LLC 2017). Since her book went to print, Lauren has had further achievements and has shared some here. She lives in her hometown of Durham, North Carolina, and can be found online at breakfast-etc.com.

listening to a party from my bed like who am I. this isn't who I am, just breaking all the time, just collecting seconds on each lap to see if I can end up.

I feel ok, but I'm lying. I finally read your book, except I didn't—I just held it to my chest like a small child. I am followed up the stairs to my door, to my new green fortress. there are pink roses outside my window, even in november—still, I haven't set foot outside. I don't know what you mean by safety—no one is safe; I've just forgotten the danger.

I answered the phone only a day after it rang. I meant things that I said; I talked too much. I'm letting myself whatever I want, a little daydream or desire and a touch of indifference. I gave it a week.

all that little motion the result of a hormonal nightmare in which I let myself, and I loved me. all this regression and nerves, when I could just put a pink rose in my hair and be in the world.

I give it a month.

HUMAN ACHIEVEMENT: FUTON

I sit and try not to accomplish anything. a better song comes on, but I am distracted. my shoulder twitches, my interest fades. my neck is sore. I add more songs. I take more pills.

somewhere in an alternate universe, I am existing, and it functions. somewhere my head is in the lion's mouth and I love it, I am begging it not to adore me. its teeth pearls around my extended throat, its saliva my new tears.

here, I fight offense at every turn. nothing allows me in. I turn a hasty, shaky cheek. once I stacked books like bricks, made oil paint moats, sewed all those doorways shut. I windexed the windows in case an airplane fell. at night, my ribcage swelled with heart-preservation in mind—even before breasts, I assumed my chest could hold up buildings if I filled it full enough. there is yet no test for this.

but there, I am serpentine and vicious. I have moonlike eyes and a breezy tongue, I have seduced empires to the ground. I smile when I am angry. when the pit of my stomach is feeling generous, I build skyscrapers and grind my teeth to hold their sway. at night, I sleep soundly and have reason to fear nothing.

SWIMMING
LESSONS

i did it again this morning
tried that daydream where
i belong inside another body
and feel so light
i swim without considering i'll drown
and comb my hair without the rip

i don't decide which escape i love best
that old head in a book
of my illustrious youth
or the swirl and burn after hours in the next bar
something bites me on the ankle and i
swat at it absently

if i am paying attention
i strike ten seconds after the boy
which tolled for me and now wants silence
at my call a bottle full of oh no
i didn't mean

what i loved about the mornings was survival
what the morning asked for amounted to defeat

THE LINGERS

i could dig holes in mountainsides all day
there are wells deeper than my eyes
how many men drowned in shallow water

every time the needle insists we should get together
then the parades over wooden bridges   have i said
anything to make you stay
recurring cases
of the lingers plague my days   late mornings
and blurred evenings preceding
                         suitcases
flung down stairs unbroken dishes safely in
their cabinets or the dishwasher even we
undisheveled   and if i pout   it is as if the lights
have gone out   we sit in the dark holding candles
unlit until i get my face fixed

the grinder working good   the burner warming up
our hands tucked in woolen hats   drafts
and cracks in workmanship   i've turned my ship
around and around aiming and avoiding for yours
for hours   if the rudder breaks it's okay the currents
are wiser and i am fine if i sleep on the float
                         i've a fainting couch
just for these ideas   rare sunlight burning the screens

HUMAN ACHIEVEMENT: MASTERY

I close my eyes and turn you into something I can conquer, something I can throw into my bag and fondle on the subway ride home. my aching feet say I work too hard. I've been out of touch. I want nightmares that show me some of this matters. I'm not ready to size up or settle where I stand. you are the least of what I love, but I love magnificently. something else gives me directions up the mountainside, no one knows what for. you go about your business. no one cares for the witch I found in my mirror, the trail of annoyances and awkward puffs of air I leave in my wake. I used to have othervision. I used to see right through people. now just the breaks. now just the train run off the tracks.◑

THE UNTITLED

Words by Jennifer Hayler
Photography by Brendon Burton

Jennifer Hayler was born and raised in the Willamette Valley. She graduated with a degree in Film Studies and lives in Portland, Oregon with her husband. The Untitled is her first fiction publication.

One day the man made a mistake.

"Shoot," he said, and looked over his shoulder, but no one was there.

For lunch, he ate a tuna fish sandwich. When he finished, he put his hand on his belly with contentment and leaned back in the plastic chair. He looked up at the break room clock. Five minutes left before he needed to return to his desk. As he watched the second-hand complete another circle, a whoosh fell in the pit of his stomach, like rotten floorboards giving way. He sat up and steadied himself at the edge of the small table. Just the tuna fish, he thought. Delicious, but temperamental.

The IT department moved like a band of thugs throughout the office, always on the lookout for trouble. It was common to see them pile into a tiny cubicle to do little more than berate the poor weak-minded employee whose job was to sit there all day.

But now they were wordless and busy with movement. The man stood at the opening of his own tiny cubicle and watched as IT tore up cords and cables like stalks from a dying garden. One of them stopped and sniffed the air; they all turned.

"So," one said, "you're here."

The man's shock lifted, replaced by a spark of annoyance. They were always so condescending. But there was no use in fighting, so he asked if he could help with anything.

"Doubtful," said one, as they reached for the printer.

Another one with eyes as flat and dark as a swamp said, "We got orders to rip and roll."

It was true. His computer was being taken apart and piled onto a cart.

"I don't understand," said the man, and he thought briefly of the mistake. But he knew he was powerless. No one ever stood up against IT, especially if they had orders. All the man could do was watch as his computer became less and less like his computer and more and more like distantly familiar junk.

They finished without another word and wheeled the cart away. The man re-entered his cubicle. Just like normal, he told himself and sat down. But it was not normal. It was as if a small tornado

landed, took only the necessary items, and left. He picked up a few stray paperclips and put them back into their holder.

The office was loud, a mush of chatter, but from inside each cubicle one could feel totally alone, totally invisible. His head fell to its most natural position, staring at the now empty spot where his computer had been. Don't worry, he thought, and looked at the blank walls of his cubicle. The fabric was a subtle chaotic mixture of blues, black, and grey. No pattern.

This was a crisis. Fortunately, the man prided himself at being good in a crisis. Last summer, for example, the paper towel dispenser broke in the bathroom and it took five months for management to fix it. Everyone walked around confused with wet hands. The man, though, brought a towel from home and carried it with him rolled under his arm. It became a trend. Everyone carried towels. People slung them around their necks or wore them all day on a shoulder like an accessory. Rowdy types snapped them at interns and ran away laughing. The whole office felt like a gym but people were happy. The crisis was handled. The man thought of his leadership during that time with a humble fondness. He smiled.

Despite this reverie and the omnidirectional lighting overhead, the man felt a shadow fall upon his shoulder. A moment later his chair was yanked backward, and he was pulled into the aisle. IT was back. There was a jumble of movement. His paperclip holder was knocked over, spilling paperclips again. Then he saw it: the sleek coxed-up form of a brand new computer.

The man rose to his feet. "What's this?" he asked.

"It's a refurb," said one of the IT wiping the brushed aluminum casing with a cloth.

THE MAN THOUGHT OF HIS LEADERSHIP DURING THAT TIME WITH A HUMBLE FONDNESS.

"Am I the only one getting one?"

They didn't answer him, but he knew.

IT finished and filed out of the cubicle. One of them slapped him on the back as they left.

The man reentered his cubicle as if it was a sacred shrine and sat down in his chair. He cupped his hand over the mouse and skated it briefly across the pad. The monitor lit up and the crisp image of some mountain, draped in fog and beauty, appeared on the screen. Just then someone passed by, Debbie...or Donna...or Sharon, he couldn't remember. She turned and scrunched her thickly penciled eyebrows together, definitely interested. She looked at him and smiled. The man felt an ember of pride. It was a very nice computer, nicer, for sure, than his co-workers' computers. It seemed that, perhaps, there was something inherently special about him. The man rode this feeling until 5 o'clock, filing reports and sending messages faster than usual.

Traffic on his way home was not so bad. He passed the familiar scenery without noticing any of it: chunks of concrete followed by chunks of siding, giant signs advertising college or tires or God, parking lots full and barren at the same time. His mind floated above these mundane realities. Between a pregnancy announcement and the hubbub with his new computer, the office was abuzz with gossip. The words promotion and big were mentioned. The man found this titillating.

After a simple dinner of rice and stew, he put on his coat and went for a walk. He took a little flask of vodka with him and sipped it whenever he saw a crow. He would've preferred bluebirds, but they were not very common in his neighborhood.

He turned down a dead end and encountered a large number of crows, pecking at litter in the street. The specks of their eyes were invisible against the growing evening. He remembered reading somewhere that crows recognize human faces. He found that fascinating. They knew him, even though he didn't know them. The man drained the rest of his flask and returned home drunk, his skin a layer of frost, and his ears ringing with cold. He took a hot shower then went to bed and fell asleep in an instant.

Hours later he awoke in the night. Something was wrong. Shapes seemed to move in the darkness. It was his head, a dizziness. He went to the bathroom to splash his face with water. He thought about the day his wife left, claiming she couldn't stand all the little beard trimmings always sitting around the sink any longer and walked out, taking their little dog, Grapefruit, with her. He still thought about that image: Grapefruit smiling at him from over his wife's shoulder as the door closed between him and them forever.

The man returned to the bedroom, sat at the edge of his mattress, and held onto his knees. Sometimes it felt as if there was a thick metal coil pressed inside of him, exerting a force he could barely contain. He thought of his new computer. That was something. That made him happy. He was sweating, his heart was beating very fast, and now a sharp ache crept through his body, down his back and arms. He thought of his mistake; there was more than one, it seemed. He thought of his brother who lived three states over. It had been many years since they spoke. The man picked up the phone. It would be morning there, and he hoped to catch him before work. It rang and rang but there was no answer. After hanging up, the man sat and waited for something to happen. In his house it was still very dark.

SOMETIMES IT FELT AS IF THERE WAS A THICKMETAL COIL PRESSED INSIDE OF HIM, EXERTING A FORCE HE COULD BARELY CONTAIN.

Okay, he thought. Okay, okay, okay.

XXXXXX

When he arrived at his cubicle the next morning, management was there holding a meeting.

"Look," they told him, "this cubicle has been promoted."

The man remained silent but shot a worried glance to the new computer. Management noticed this, and an awkward look passed among them. They handed him an envelope. Inside it, there were two pieces of paper: a coupon for large nachos at a restaurant chain and a notice of termination. He looked at the notice in disbelief.

"We can't tell you much, seeing as you no longer work here. But your cubicle is perfect for our needs."

There were a number of nods and murmurs, "Yes, yes."

"Remarkable cubicle," added another.

They handed him a cardboard box. He looked inside and it was empty.

"It's just a formality. We didn't find any of your personal belongings."

As he walked away, the man felt all the eyes in the office watching him, pitying him, or maybe just glad it wasn't them.

Outside, he passed the IT department. They were on break, leaning against the wall and smoking.

"Why didn't anyone tell me?" he asked.

One of them spat. "Tell you what?"

"That I was fired. That the computer wasn't for me."

He looked for a sympathetic face among them, but the sun was rising behind the building and their faces were smudged by shadow.

"Is it the job of the foot to clap?" they asked. "Is it the job of the mouth to think?"

One of them offered him a cigarette and the man took it, but no one offered him a match, so he just held it at his side.

"My cubicle was promoted. They called it remarkable." The man felt very sad as he said this.

"Well, that's probably it then," one of them said, and there was a lot more spitting.

Then another leaned forward. "Maybe you need to expand your horizons. Find something new. When a door closes and all that. The world has a lot to offer, you know."

The man took his unlit cigarette and left. He hated the IT department.

He walked and walked, down streets he recognized and then down streets he did not recognize at all. He hopped a metal railing and walked along a dirt road he never walked down before. The landscape was dreary, in every direction flat dull foliage. The man looked up. Power-lines on tall oily poles skimmed across the grey sky, out into somewhere. His eyes followed them and then his legs. The man stayed on the dirt road even as it narrowed into a path, even as it narrowed further, only a hint between the grass.

He found a dead crow in a field. It was perfectly intact. Its wings were spread wide open. He looked at it very closely. How beautifully the black feathers lay over each other.

"I'm sorry," he said to the crow. "I don't think I recognize you."

He sat down. He was sweating, and the oxygen did not pass easily through the constricting paths inside him.

"I'm sorry," he said again, feeling like a small, empty cup bobbing in a great cold ocean. ❶

66

TOKYO FREE TIME

Words by Craig Foster
Illustration by Wooden Cyclops

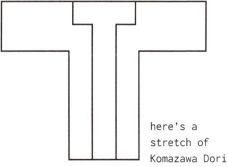

here's a stretch of Komazawa Dori the yakimo vendors avoid. It starts near the train station, where the free-timers hand out facial tissue packets advertising mobile phone deals, and ends several blocks away close to the shrine. Raw yakimo are cheap at the station's market, and incense escaping the shrine masks the smell of them roasting over wood fires burning on the vendors' truck beds. The threat of an explosion lurks but the yakimo are always worth it.

The vendors and their trucks mostly stick to the interior streets. Just residents. Little competition.

A fog of pink lanterns hovers over the plaza that fronts the station. The Setsubun festival that always celebrates spring much too early has happened already, with cries of Oni wa soto! Fuku wa uchi! (Demons out! Luck in!) having died in the streets weeks earlier. It's cold season and

the free-timers are running out of tissue
packets. Some slow down the handouts,
stretching what passes for work hours
as best as possible. The ones dressed
for later fun practically toss them into
the crowd. Nothing moves quickly enough
for them.

A soothing recorded voice announces the
arrival of a train and they all gear up
for another stream of people. A few move
closer to the exit, thanking the commuters
for taking the free gift before it's
even handed over. A reeling salaryman,
face blown red with drink, crashes through
a turnstile and knocks a hand clutching
tissues, sending packets flying. The
free-timer apologizes a bit too loudly
and the commuter, taken aback, turns
toward her. The moment drains some of
the blood from his face, almost erasing
the deep flush below his eyes. He doesn't
know whether to offer an apology in kind
or let her continue to express regret for
her role in his mistake. He drops his
eyes to her shoes. These are massive
platforms plastered with peeling stickers
of both The Bathing Ape and an aging
American singer who's enjoying renewed
popularity this year thanks to a TV ad
for an over-the-counter gastrointestinal
relief tablet. Seeing the free-timer's
feet so high above the ground reminds
him of a time when he floated through the
old neighborhood, roller-skating
alongside his dog. Those weren't great
years either, but thinking of skimming
just a little above the pavement, toward
the train tracks and along the levee,
makes his lip twitch toward a smile.

The other commuters have moved past him.
It seems time has, too. He picks up the
one tissue package not yet gathered by
the free-timer, who with each shout
makes clear there is no real apology
behind this at all. He raises the package
to his forehead, bows slightly toward
her, conjures one last image of the dog,
turns toward the plaza, and steps into
the street.

When the company publishes his obituary
a few days later, there is no mention of
how he died. How a yakimo vendor who'd
been uncharacteristically driving near
the station struck him down. Instead,
it tells of years of commitment, focus,
and consistency. Of the time he gave
that speech. Of the joke he told all
the new interns.

The vendor sends a basket of perfect
yakimo, which the head of HR places on
an altar near the elevator. Everyone
takes out a tissue when they stand near
it, for the first couple of days.●

THE OTHER COMMUTERS HAVE MOVED PAST HIM. IT SEEMS TIME HAS, TOO.

DISPOSABLE MEMORIES

An Interview with Corbin Corbin
By Raechel Wolfe

Corbin is a rare breed. He holds down a typical office job while making time to participate in the arts and support the Portland community. While attending house shows, tenants' rights rallies, Blue Collar Wrestling matches, or even just walking down the street, Corbin takes pictures with cheap disposable cameras he buys in bulk online. What's come from his obsession with documenting everything is a staggering collection of photographs capturing the moments of thousands of strangers, forming a running visual diary of Portland.

MY FAMILY WASN'T ARTSY IN ANY WAY, BUT CAMERAS WERE THE ONE THING THAT WERE CONSISTENTLY AROUND THE HOUSE.

Why did you start documenting everything you see?

C: I've been taking the same kind of photo forever. I can dig up pictures I took at parties I threw in High School, which conceptually are not too dissimilar from pictures that I take at parties I throw now—stacks of empty cans, except back then they were soda cans, and of people hanging out having fun. I really like to document stuff. My dad likes to take pictures, not like a ton, but he had cameras I could play with. My family wasn't artsy in any way, but cameras were the one thing that were consistently around the house. I think the image that sticks around in my head a lot is the cultural meme of the great aunt and uncle that go on vacation and they make you sit there and watch their slideshows—that is my inspiration! Being that relative that makes you sit there. Fortunately, mine are on Facebook and people can watch from the comfort of their own home.

Why do you choose to use disposable cameras?

C: I've gone through lots of different cameras over the years, but I would use disposables occasionally at parties. I'd pick one up if I was going to New York for a long weekend and we were going to be partying in my friend's hotel. I'd use the camera and then I'd be done with it for a while. In the Spring of 2014 I was going to some party and I wanted to take a disposable camera with me. I went to a Walgreens to buy one and they were 12 bucks a piece, which is stupid. I bought a camera for that night, thinking that would be the last time I ever used a disposable camera. I thought if this is what they cost I can't casually buy these garbage cameras. I ended up going on eBay and found 32 cameras for 48 dollars, which is a crazy deal, far cheaper than you would ever find normally. I bought those just to save money, not because I needed the cameras, and I very much thought at the time that I will have those cameras for the rest of my life. I would use maybe one or two a year - I guess I thought I would die in fifteen years! Once I had a box of them, I decided I would keep one in my pocket, just in case I would run into somebody on the street, which I would do frequently, and then it went from there.

I'm happy for the "Juggalos are comrades" awakening.

These are serious competitors at the International Cat Show - best stay out of their way.

My friend put on this show called "Ol' Eyez Never Die" at the music box village in New Orleans, a very cool and unique venue/playground.

Purple Burple Man makes an appearance at a Toxic Slime Records show - always a crowd favorite!

How has your content evolved over time?
C: I don't think of myself as a photographer
or a music photographer or any of that—I just
like to go to shows and I have the camera in
my pocket. At some point, I recognized that
people were engaging [on Facebook] with the
band pictures more than the pictures of people
standing around, so I figured I should [organize]
them in a separate place so that they stand on
their own.

**Do you find that having a camera helped
you engage with people? Does it help to
have an activity to do in a place where
you didn't know anyone?**
C: It depends on the environment. I like having
a camera at shows because it's an excuse to
stand in the front, which is ultimately what
I want to do more than I want to take pictures
because that's the best place to have a good
time. I generally try to keep [the cameras] in
my pocket. I'm not trying to advertise that I'm
the person with the camera. Sometimes, I'll
take one out and set it on the table and wait
for someone to remark on it if I'm at a place
where I don't know anyone. Often someone won't
have seen one in a while and will come up and
comment on it, and then we'll talk.

**You mentioned not wanting to advertise that you
are the "man with the camera" but that is how
you are recognized across many scenes in
Portland, and beyond.**
C: That's fine, but to me that's incidental.
It's certainly not on purpose. I like when I
can meet people and they don't know I'm a person
with a camera. In getting into conversations,
I've found that people have formed their own
ideas on what I'm doing and why. A lot of people
don't know I'm using disposable cameras—they
think I'm using a real camera. I've encountered
people who think I'm getting paid, which, I'm
like, who exactly do you think is paying me to
photograph my own life?

One of Vancouver, BC's Vörös Twins taking a bottle at DOA Pro Wrestling at the Boys & Girls Club in SE. DOA is just one of Portland's multiple local wrestling promos.

The mysteriously masked musicians of Kulululu have never revealed their identities - who could they be?

Somebody invited me to this music video shoot for the song "Say My Name" by Summer Cannibals. This is the lead singer. You can see me at the 1:00 mark.

What pictures or scenes are you most fond of capturing?

C: I recognize the band pictures are the ones that people are most aware of. Sometimes I resent the band pictures because I like the other pictures more and people are only looking at the band pictures. People don't like the pictures I like, for the most part. That's why I don't like to curate my own stuff. I have my own biases.

Are you documenting the scene or are you creating the scene? A lot of people could point to your pictures and say, "This is Portland" or "This is what Portland looks like". How true is the story you are telling?

C: It's what happens in Corbin's life. That's what all this comes down to, that's all the pictures are, my life and experiences. It's a wholly selfish work. It's proof that it happened for my future self that lacks the ability to remember anymore. Or for descendants or whatever. I'm just hanging out. I'm just a roaming fan. There's plenty of bands and people who I'm the only person who's taken a picture of them in years. If there's no other content being produced, it's easy to seem like it's representing something larger than it is, because there are no other visuals of some of this stuff. And I think people who aren't involved in this but are Facebook friends with me can consume a lot of this and make up their own ideas about what it means and what it is.

I DON'T THINK THAT THIS TIME IS ANY MORE IMPORTANT THAN WHAT CAME BEFORE OR WHAT WILL COME AFTER.

Do you think that sometime in the future you are going to look back on this body of work and this time of your life and see a larger theme and meaning?

C: Other people have brought this to me, like "One day there's going to be a documentary about the Portland music scene and this era and they are gonna use your pictures…" Uh, I don't know… sure! I don't think that this time is any more important than what came before or what will come after. House shows were going on long before I started taking pictures of them. I'm just capturing now.

Stanley jams out at the Lost House at the DUG 3-year anniversary (Check out @deepunderground on Instagram!)

May Day 2017. This is when things started to get hairy - police were quick to escalate.

This is my backyard, but I don't really remember having a Halloween party.

A rare performance by Granny Gums. I had already left the room before this happened but ran back inside when I heard shouting, and got there just in time.

You are out participating in the art, music, wrestling, political, and just about every other cultural happening that you can attend in a given week. What do you think about the "Old Portland" vs. "New Portland" grumblings?

C: I think it's short-sighted. There's always been a "New Portland". Portland has always been a place of new transplants. I don't like nativism of any sort, but I think nativism of Portland is especially silly because people just don't have that much claim to duration here. I'm more concerned with how one interacts with the city and what they bring to it. I meet new people all the time who moved to Portland to get involved in the music scene, and after a while, they are hosting house shows. There's nothing wrong with that. The local person who turns up their nose at someone who's new and complains about things without going out and interacting with the city themselves, I don't care about them.

I think that people tend to slip into the mindset that whatever they know is all there is. I've been to house shows where people will say "God, there hasn't been a house show in months, there's never house shows anymore," and I'm like, I was at another house show an hour ago and I'm going to another one tomorrow. You feel that way because YOUR friends don't have house shows, and your friends stopped playing music. That doesn't mean everyone did. A lot of people come to Portland to make music and to make art. There's four house shows tonight that I'm aware of, and that means there's at least five. The more I'm out there, the more I realize how little I know. There are always new places popping up.

I THINK THAT PEOPLE TEND TO SLIP INTO THE MINDSET THAT WHATEVER THEY KNOW IS ALL THERE IS.

Do you see yourself continuing on with documenting life with disposable cameras for a while?

C: I don't know, it's like a curse at this point. A compulsion. I scout around on eBay to find good deals and when I don't find them I think "Uh, this is gonna get costly because I'm gonna have to keep paying for this stupid thing". I don't know if I even like doing it. It just happens.

Spaghetti the duck was cautious at first, even hostile, but he warmed up and became quite friendly.
Sadly, his life was cut short by a nighttime beast. He was a soft and good duck.

GUN, and the eponymous gun-turned-microphone

Whenever I take pictures of singers, I aim for the open mouth, so you can tell they're singing.
This is Leona from Mr Wrong belting one out.

The International Cat Show is a great way to see some of the best that this beloved species has to offer!

Dr. Doom networking at the Oregon Historical Society; this is one of my favorite pictures.

Do you have any plan to show or do anything with this large amount of content you've created?
C: If people want to ask me to do something with it, I will probably do it. There's an art gallery in town that opened up not long ago, and the curator told me I'm the inspiration behind their next exhibit which is going to be all disposable camera focused. That will be the first time I'll have anything on a wall. I've been in some zines before… There's just a lot of fuckin' pictures! Last year I took about three thousand pictures. I don't know what I would want to focus on. To me, the sheer quantity of them is the most significant thing. I would want to do a show focused on that. I have some ideas of what I would do if I had some space and budget to work with. Oh, and someone else to do all the work, haha! I'd rather go hang out.. **Ⓑ**

You can follow Corbin's adventures by finding him on Facebook, or following on Instagram at @corbincorbin

AXIS/PRAXIS

Words by E.L. Hopkins
Digital Artwork by Braeden Cox

E.L. Hopkins is a Texas-born writer whose
international popularity is rivaled only by
his stunning physical beauty. Though best
known for his award-winning fiction, Hopkins
is also an amateur marksman and illusionist,
specializing in shooting himself in the foot
and making money disappear.

"THE IMAGE IN THESE OPENING LINES EVIDENTLY REFERS TO A BIRD KNOCKING ITSELF OUT…"

-PROF. CHARLES KINBOTE IN PALE FIRE, NABOKOV

fell in love with Alex when I saw her shoplifting vodka in the middle of the day. She was beautiful and dangerous and exciting, like an alcoholic Russian spy with no mission and a lot of free time. She claimed to have once been a champion junior figure skater, and described a childhood that would be aptly filmed on the rugged steppes and Ural prominence of that forbidding country.

Our marriage and subsequent problems began almost immediately. *Par exemple*: I could never quite shake the feeling that she was in fact a Russian spy. That she would become openly hostile whenever I accused her of this was either some kind of Ophelian confession (the lady doth protest too much, and with much too efficient violence), or possibly she was tired of the subject *in toto*, and each time I re-tabled it (often) was like another arrow through poor Gabriel's already well-ventilated chest.

There was also an unfortunate incident when, in a pique of nameless rage, she claimed that not only was my mere presence deeply upsetting, but even worse, that my speech and prose style were both ridiculous. The fact that either one of us was still willing to marry the other is a testament to the incurability of the human condition.

After leaving me, Alex discovered an endless queue of men whose eagerness to defile her body she mistook for passion. The most passionate was my accountant, who flung himself into this new project with the same revolting gusto he'd once reserved for defrauding his clients. Namely: me. He soon learned that my wife's pseudo-bohemian/pseudo-political loathing for money stood in stark contrast to her all too authentic love of things that only money can provide, and her new mark provided all of these things with my money, until it ran out.

I've always thought of memories as little poison pills that taste sweet at first but are actually designed to burn holes through your insides. The happier the memory, the more potent its poison. Fortunately, I have very few happy memories waiting like snipers in the trees of my mind. The happiest memory I have (redacted) is like a red-hot poker plunged directly into the core of my being. (Please forgive this crude metaphorical stew, I have an excruciating headache and there seems to be a marching band practicing somewhere in the vicinity of my hippocampus.)

In my experience the best antidote to memories is wealth.

Being rich is wonderful in pretty much every way (better food, conventionally attractive prostitutes), but fame is something else. Being adored. The most charming thing about being adored is avoiding those who adore you: in my case the general public, who were awakened to my genius with the release of my best selling novel (The Likeness) six years ago, and have subsequently been haunting me ever since. Which is why I built this fortress, this kingdom on the water.

But I didn't
count on the
loneliness.
Loneliness is,
for a person who
hates other people,
a strange and confusing
thing. Even extremely expensive
prostitutes can only provide so much insulation
against the chills of loneliness, especially when
they accuse you of "talking funny" and then
abscond in the middle of the night with a certain
rare and priceless book you were generous enough
to show them (more on that later).

When I woke up here alone and savagely hungover
this gray morning in the height of gray season,
without my book, I was inconsolable. I felt
like burning my house down for warmth and
walking into the lake to cool down.

After buying the lakefront property, I
immediately burned down the house that had
been there. The very moment of purchase
actually, with the vacated family still huddled
in the driveway watching the ink dry on my
check. I'll never forget the stunned look on
their faces or the naked awe that scintillated
in their tiny vitamin-deficient eyes as their
memories vanished in a truly magnificent
conflagration. I then hired a supposedly promising
young architect to build my dream fortress.
I had very concrete notions of what I wanted,
with features and details that at times seemed
to mystify my fraudulent tyro in their specificity
and apparent "eccentricity." I for one didn't
find it the least bit eccentric to want rifle
turrets on all four corners of a home that in

appearance had more in common with a futuristic castle than a house. If he'd understood what suffering I've known—what mournful arias have rattled the clammy viscera of my soul—he would've understood my need for security. My need to feel martial in my solitude. So we had to part ways, not without considerable hostility on his part. Apparently, he not only wanted to be paid for his failure but also thought he deserved additional compensation for the duration and intensity of our encounters. All this, according to the court summons and subsequent restraining order he attempted to levy against me.

Staring through bloodshot eyes at the gray lake and the gray trees and the gray geese flocking stupidly among the cattails, two or three silk kimonos clutched around my neck, I forgot how to breathe. I needed to go outside and be there with the ugliness. I needed a change of attire.

As the chip-activated exterior door slid closed behind me with a satisfying pneumatic hiss I'd paid good money for, I noticed a pair of dead birds crumpled on the ground at the foot of my western wall, which they had obviously crashed into. Their feathers were ruffled and gunked up with brain juice and immediately I felt somewhat better. I appreciated the respite, however temporary, from the bitter knowledge of my missing book. People say that cats and wind turbines kill the most birds, but they've never seen my fortress. They've never witnessed the awesome avian annihilating power of its merciless slate gray façade, which blends seamlessly with the sky on certain days and takes down birds like mad Ajax sacrificing sheep. It's been suggested to me—at times hysterically—that I should have the house repainted, presumably to spare the birds. I always answer the same: It's not a house, it's a fortress. A castle. And no I won't have it repainted. Both because I like the color (which is obviously why I chose it),

LONELINESS IS, FOR A PERSON WHO HATES OTHER PEOPLE, A STRANGE AND CONFUSING THING.

and because I hate birds and lose no sleep over their deaths. The more the better, I say. I've hated birds ever since my best friend of childhood chased a rebellious parrot into the road and was destroyed by a moving truck. People ask me with their stupid grins, *You must hate moving trucks as well, then,* trying to snare me in some logical inconsistency. It's amusing for a living bundle of contradictions such as myself to watch those with a low functioning cognitive apparatus attempt to make sense of my actions. I assure you, it is not possible. Some of the finest clinical minds of my time have made it their sole obsession to understand me, most of them dying before making even a cursory analysis (some passing naturally, some otherwise). My triumph over these people is a fait accompli.

And yes: of course I also hate moving trucks.

I walked down to the edge of the water, kicking loose stones as I went, thinking about red pandas. I always think about red pandas when I'm upset. Standing near the water gazing up at my castle was a sad-faced college-aged male with a vaguely Russian looking gray spotted dog. One of the stones I kicked inadvertently struck the animal on a hind leg and it let out a piercing screech that echoed across the lake. I would've apologized, but I was too deep in personal misery. It must be acknowledged that extraordinarily wealthy geniuses have problems that can't be understood by the unwashed masses, and that we don't always have the time or leisure to worry about animals that we may or may not have struck with stones. Because of my overwhelming magnanimity, however, I managed to thumb off a couple dollars from the wad in my pocket and toss them as near to the wounded beast as I could without risking a conversation with its master. My heart was broken and I wasn't in the mood to be adulated. Not by another man, anyway. It has far too often been the case that men who claim sexual attraction solely to women turn out to be rather tenuous in that regard once they've made my acquaintance. I can hardly blame them, but nor can I entertain them.

I was nearly halfway around the lake when the sky grew dark and threatening and I felt the first of what soon became a torrent of generously proportioned raindrops. I hadn't worn my slicker and within moments my wool sweater and tweed trousers were drenched and heavy, forcing me to adopt a parody of ambulatory movement, kicking each leg out in front of me as if at invisible enemies. Then I started to imagine that I really was kicking my enemies and swung my legs with increasing velocity and malevolence.

I was deep in meditation and didn't immediately hear the man's voice calling out to me.

"Are you okay?" the voice said, and I became retroactively aware that it had already asked me this at least six times.

"I'm fine!" I bellowed, scanning my immediate environs hawkishly but unable to divine the source of the intrusion.

"I'm up here." The voice said, with a bit more hilarity than seemed necessary or appropriate.

Glancing up the slow root-gnarled rise off the lake to the modest dwelling perched there, I saw a man watching me, holding the collar of a familiar looking spotted dog. Staggering up the muddy slope to make a more thorough appraisal of my interlocutor and his beast, I slipped and went down face first, gashing my elbow on a rock and losing both my glasses and my pistol. Clawing fruitlessly through the mud in which I was now completely ensconced, I silently cursed the man and his dog and the lake and my

AND YES: OF COURSE I ALSO HATE MOVING TRUCKS.

parents and my neighbors growing up. Eventually, I remembered that I hadn't been wearing my glasses and after abandoning the pistol I solemnly rose to my full height of six feet and four inches and continued my trek up the increasingly treacherous slope. As I approached, the man took a quick step back and the dog cowered between his legs. Probably it had been so long since the animal had enjoyed the company of an alpha that it wasn't sure how to react.

"Are you okay?" the man asked yet again, a faint grin hovering in the vicinity of his face. I wanted to shoot him and would have if not for obvious reasons.

"Yes, I'm still fine." I said icily, extending my hand for the obligatory violence of a shake.

Looking at my muddy appendage and the blood that was dripping from my elbow down my sleeve onto his deck, he grimaced and shook his head.

"Better not." He said. "I've been a bit under the weather, and I'd hate to pass it on."

"Well thank you for that." I said, sheathing my digits. "The last thing I need is to add some nondescript peasant disease to my already impressive litany of hardships."

"You must be the writer." He said.

Good lord, I thought, not another one.

"Yes, that's true." I admitted. "I live across the lake. I'm sure you've seen my fortress. I've been told it's impossible to miss, no matter how hard you try to miss it."

"What lake?" the man asked, screwing up his face as if trying to solve a math problem in his head.

"What do you mean, what lake?" I asked, flinging a muddy and incredulous hand in the appropriate direction. "The lake. What other lake could I possibly be referring to?" I often swam in the lake, always a cavalier in the nude despite the threat of water snakes, which frighten me more than anything on Earth (unfortunate sunbathing incident in childhood). I'd been assured there was no such threat in this northwestern region of the United States, but you can't believe anything people say about anything.

The man looked in the direction indicated and blinked expressionlessly. Then his eyes brightened and a repellent smile swept across his features.

"The lake!" he laughed, clapping his minuscule pink hands. "Of course. I guess it is kind of a lake. That's funny."

"I don't see what's so funny about it." I said, and was prepared to launch an oral history of the lake and its stark seriousness, but was rudely interrupted.

"Actually I've been meaning to stop by for a quick chat." The man said. "I've just been so busy. I recently bought a restaurant, you see, and…"

"You bought a restaurant? Why not invest in floppy disks and dinosaur bones?" I asked him. "You should've just bought a boat. At least then you'd have a nice place to kill yourself."

His smile diminished appreciably and he muttered something about the questionable legality of my bathing habits.

"What are you, some kind of lawyer?" I demanded. "Some kind of pimp!?"

"What? No, I…just wanted…"

"Because you should know that I don't entertain my readers, and I certainly don't entertain lawyers and pimps."

"I'm none of those, actually." He lied, his tone growing churlish. "I'm just a man whose son you antagonized and whose dog you hit with a rock and who's tired of listening to his wife complain about the naked person across the pond."

"Well I'm sorry for your marital discord," I told him. "But I don't see what it has to do with me."

"It has everything to do with you."

"How in the world do you figure? Nevermind," I scolded him, "I don't have time for this nonsense. Life is short, and thanks to you mine is even shorter now."

Turning to go I slipped and fell down the gnarly slope to the water, lacerating my back on byzantine root structures, knocking the wind out of me. I gasped. I writhed. What's happened to me? What's happened to my world? My book?

My book: for virtually all of recorded human history it has been the secret delight of the global elite to commission realistic portraiture of their own fundaments, with specific regard to the sphincter; it so happens that I own one of the only compiled anthologies of these works of art—some of which transcend the others in terms of subject, technical merit, and objective beauty. Not everyone seems to love the book as much as I do, and are consequently ignorant of certain historical facts they would never learn elsewhere. For example, would you believe that Marie Antoinette had a small mole resting

daintily in the umbra northeast of her unusually dark star, like a black dwarf orbiting a supernova? Or that the Baroness de Rothschild had such a dense accumulation of follicles that for her portrait to be successfully rendered a team of stylists worked in concert for the better part of an afternoon, using clothespins to free from obstruction her frankly massive orifice and its vast epidermic shadow? Or that despite his profound lust for unhygienic women, Napoleon's own anus was bleached so thoroughly and capriciously that he spent most of his adult life in constant and excruciating rectal pain? Which explains a lot. Virtually no one knows these facts but me. But do people appreciate my divestment of such wealth? No, they do not. The only person who ever showed sufficient interest in such matters was my former accountant, with whom I can no longer enjoy conversing for obvious reasons.

Just as the rain stopped I saw my neighbor's wife come out of her house and walk under a low trellis into her garden. The new trellis was so low, in fact, that with my extraordinary height I find it uncomfortable to fold myself under it, and am therefore effectively excluded from the garden. A fact that bothers Mrs. Bishop less than it should.

By the time I breached the lakeside portico, crawling on all fours, she was already on her hams inspecting something or other, her newborn in a wicker bassinette at her side. When she finally looked up and saw me entombed in my mud carapace, bleeding from several locations, she screamed like she'd witnessed a murder. Once she realized what she was dealing with her expression of horror relaxed into a grimace. When she's not grimacing it's possible to discern the classic Russian beauty Mrs. Bishop must've once possessed. However, she never stops grimacing.

"Some rain." I said, struggling to my feet.

Mrs. Bishop looked up at the sky, which was now as clear and blue as my eyes would've been if they weren't covered in filth.

"It was raining until a moment ago." I assured her. She didn't seem to believe me. She's a

WHAT'S HAPPENED TO ME? WHAT'S HAPPENED TO MY WORLD? MY BOOK?

difficult woman and has never forgiven me for
destroying a significant quantity of her roses
one night.

"I wasn't hiding," I said, to distract her from
the fact that I'd been hiding. "I just thought
that I saw a snake in the shrub and didn't want
it to attack your baby."

"Why would a snake attack my daughter?"

"Because your daughter is precisely who I would
attack!" I said a bit too enthusiastically,
quickly adding, "If I were a snake."

We shared a pregnant moment of silence.

"Sorry again about your roses." I said, gesturing
at the decimated corner patch where I'd crashed
my bicycle. "Though it looks like you still
have plenty."

More silence.

"So," Mrs. Bishop said when she realized I wasn't
going to leave. "Seeing anyone?" It was obvious
she was interested in neither my response nor my
romantic life.

"Nyet." I said, thinking of my priceless book.
"It's not worth it."

"How do you mean?"

"I mean it in every possible way."

Mrs. Bishop nodded slowly, furtively wielding
a garden trowel.

My friend was apparently not home. Most likely
he was on his way over to my place to raid my
liquor, though his wife strenuously assured me
this wasn't the case. I considered inviting
myself in to dry off, but as if anticipating

97

the offer Mrs. Bishop informed me that she'd
locked herself out of the house and was waiting
for her husband to come home and let her in.
The fact that her back door was ajar and that
I noticed a conspicuous flutter of a curtain
from the upstairs bathroom suggested that she
was mistaken, but I said nothing. It's not
possible to convince idiots of anything and
I seldom make the mistake of trying.

I was on the final leg of my journey, my fortress
within sight, when I encountered a college-aged
male with a dog. The dog was limping and I
had a good mind to thrash the young man for
mistreating his animal. Something about them
looked familiar. Vaguely Russian.

"Hello." The young man said.

"Do I know you?" I asked.

"You hit my dog with a rock." He said.

"You'll have to be more specific."

"An hour ago, next to the lake. You kicked a
rock and it hit my dog, and you walked off like
nothing had happened."

"Oh, right. Yes, I'm sorry about that. It
happens that I was experiencing intense grief
at that moment and couldn't be bothered with
spies or their animal familiars. You were
spying on me, yes?"

The young man was taken aback, confirming my
suspicions. But that didn't stop him from
lying to me.

"I wasn't spying." He said. "My parents bought
a place across the water. I was just taking my
dog for a walk."

"Your yuppie parents swoop down from their
ivory tower and price out the locals, eh? Drive
them right out of their homes into the cold?
Into the snow? Starving and likely pregnant,

IT'S NOT
POSSIBLE
TO CONVINCE
IDIOTS OF
ANYTHING
AND I SELDOM
MAKE THE
MISTAKE
OF TRYING.

99

only to be eaten alive by wolves and bears? How neat, and how kind. You're obviously great humanitarians."

"It's not nearly as nice as your place." The boy said.

"Well no, of course it isn't." I scoffed. "These hicks wouldn't know good architecture if it was dropped on their empty useless heads."

"I know," he said. "That's why I was looking at it."

"Aha!" I shouted, poking him in the chest with all nine of my fingers. "So you were spying on me! You should know better than to try to trick me, you freak. You pervert. You eastern-bloc Lothario! If you knew who I was you would know better than to try to trick me."

"I do know who you are." He said timidly. "I've read The Likeness at least a dozen times. It's my favorite book."

"Oh?" I asked. "Maybe you're not such a piece of shit after all. Tell you what. I lost my pistol in the mud somewhere to the south of your family's hovel. If you find it bring it over and we can play chess. I usually play with my head of security but he's…"

I remembered that Kevin was at this moment waiting for me—had been waiting for a few hours by now. When we first started playing I let him win a lot because I was afraid of breaking his spirit and thus losing an opponent. Over time this became something of a habit, and the habitual man that I am, I'm loathe to upset

the pattern, tedious as it may be. And I can tell that Kevin appreciates the company, despite his frequent proclamations to the contrary, and the dramatic sighs he produces whenever I sneak up behind him and jovially encircle my fingers around his throat.

When I looked up the young man and his maimed companion were gone. Just like Alex was gone, and my childhood friend was gone. Like my book was gone. Everything is always going away. And I'm here, remembering. I've drunk too deeply of Mnemosyne's sweet poison and now I'm so full of holes that life flows through me in a constant brutal surge, irrigating the barren fields of my mind, the muddy trenches of my worthless life.

Kicking a dead bird or two out of my path I approached my door and debated whether to make breakfast or kill myself, or perhaps some exotic combination of both. But then I saw it, within my shadow in that false azure, leaning against the feather encrusted bulletproof glass door. My book. The Anuses of Antiquity. Apparently, my felonious companion had a change of heart and brought it back, and I thought she deserved a gift for this unexpected moral correction. A dozen roses. I knew just where to find some.🄱

Graphic Narrative By Hugh Newell

Hugh Newell is a Portland based artist whose work orbits whatever cultural detritus he's obsessed with at the time, usually somewhere between crass jabs at haute couture and hard sci-fi. Probably from doing too many drugs, he sees the opportunity for narrative in everything. Hugh likes rock and roll and doing art for local bands and occasionally playing in them. He also likes dogs but does not own one.

103

MANHATTAN DOES NOT STAND UP, GET UP FOR MARLEY AND TOSH

Words by Walt Schaefer
Artwork by M3AT

In addition to a stint in the music biz, Schaefer worked as a typewriter repairman, bellman, baker, bartender, writer, intellectual property manager, and storyteller. He wrote the theater pieces, *The Existential Life and Lonesome Death of Meriwether Lewis*, and *Lounging in the Luminous Oxcart of Love*. Schaefer also co-wrote Things Chinese and *The Complete Book of Longevity*, and edited Timothy Leary's novel *Intelligence Agents*. An Atheneum Fellow at Portland's Attic Institute in 2015-16, Schaefer has studied with poets Matthew Dickman, David Biespiel and Wendy Willis. The poems in his chapbook, *Spider in the Straw* (ferrislane press), relate to his illness and recovery from prostate cancer.

Island?" We heard a voice in the hallway inquire softly.

We were hard to find. In 1972, the offices of Island Records in New York consisted of two small rooms tucked behind the elevators on the sixteenth floor of a building at 54th Street and 6th Avenue. The front room was big enough to hold an oversized round table, six canvas director chairs, and nothing else.

On this day, like most days, DK and I were seated at the round table. I was on the phone; DK was wrestling with the accounts.

In our tiny oasis, we'd tried to recreate the spirit that defined Island Records in England, where artists like Traffic, Cat Stevens, and Fairport Convention fed a surge in audiences for album-oriented music designed for FM airplay. The company's London offices were an open chaos of activity. Since the owner worked wherever he found an empty chair, everyone else did the same.

We drilled a hole in the center of our table from which a tangle of wires enabled several telephones and DK's adding machine. Because the adding machine didn't travel, DK had a permanent chair facing the door. The position of her chair made her the de facto receptionist unless she was preoccupied. Generally, she was preoccupied. She'd taken up the study of the abacus and used it to crosscheck her calculations.

"That's us," I said in answer to the voice in the hallway.

Bob Marley leaned in the door and asked again, "Island? Island Records?" The lilt in his voice was noticeable, as was a note of incredulity.

Today when I think about Bob, I envision dreadlocks arcing above his head as he dances across the stage in front of the band like an incarnate flame carried by some unseen, decidedly reckless, hand. In 1972, Bob's hair more closely resembled an overgrown thicket. It could have been a trick of backlighting, but a sharp break where the hair ended and the wall behind him began made his head look like the bas-relief of an emperor.

"You found us," I said.

Presence manifests in carriage, in shoulders, in chin, in spine. It's molecular and doesn't stop at the skin. Bob Marley stepped into the room, tipped his head back, and smiled.

I rose from my director's chair, came around the front of the desk, and shook his hand. A boy of the Midwest, my handshake by habit registered medium-high on the firmness scale. I stopped well short of a competitive grip but remained solidly within the sincerity range. Bob's handshake matched mine.

Tosh appeared behind Bob. It was more that he wasn't in the hall any longer than that he entered the office. You would say both men radiated confidence, but Bob's confidence moved before him like a phalanx, while Peter Tosh's confidence was a cylinder he stood inside of. When I reached out my hand, he took it softly and looked away. He wore dark glasses. I could not see or sense his eyes.

HE WORE DARK GLASSES. I COULD NOT SEE OR SENSE HIS EYES.

Tosh was tall, a solid six foot five. Almost a foot taller than Bob.

Behind us, Bob introduced himself to DK, sat down in the chair next to her, and asked about the abacus. She was slim as a straw with short dark hair and very large brown eyes. Those eyes conveyed opposite messages simultaneously, like traffic signs calmly showing go, caution, and stop all at once. Gullible and world-weary, her look would narrow in a way that suggested she'd heard and dismissed much better ideas than yours.

When I'd hired her, I'd been aware the two of us would have to run a music publishing operation and represent the New York hub of a dynamic English record label. I needed someone who could stay focused when oversized music business personalities showed up. I needn't have worried. She liked Nick Drake's records, but the rest of the music that surrounded her all day she barely noticed. After a year of working together, it was clear DK's absence of interest was more intriguing to musicians than my universal enthusiasm.

"Bomba-clot." Tosh said.

"Excuse me?" I asked.

"Ras-clot. Bomba-clot."

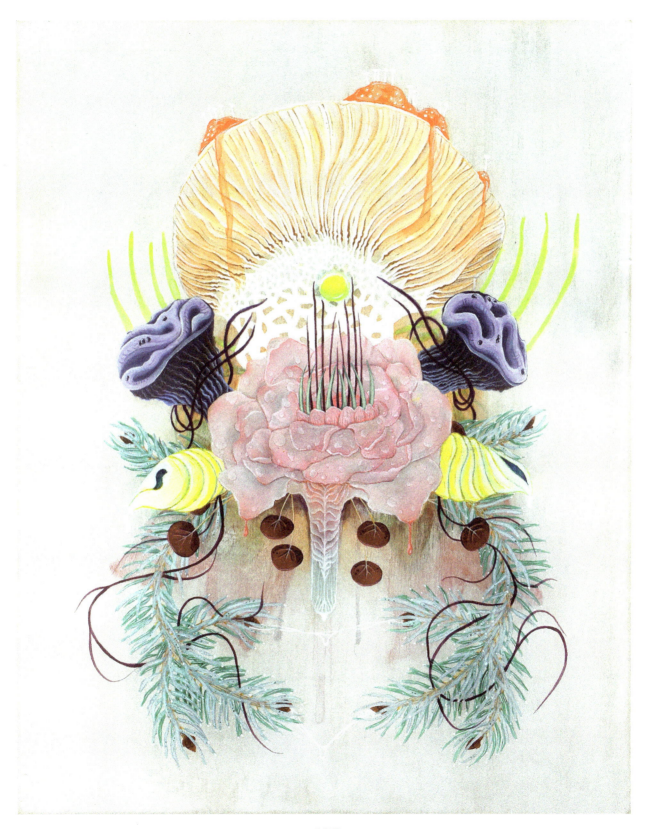

Unsure what response was called for, I blurted out, "Hey, we have an acetate of the final mix of your album." I looked at each of them in turn. "You guys are probably tired of hearing it, but I can put it on in the next room."

"Nyah. We nuh he-yard dat," Bob said softly.

I puzzled first over what he'd said. Then, when I was sure I understood him, I puzzled over how it could possibly be true.

We rarely knew when Island's owner, Chris Blackwell, would show up in the office. If we learned he was scheduled to be in New York, there was a good chance we wouldn't see him at all. Any other time, he was likely to appear. As a person subject to sometimes crippling bouts of shyness, I've studied how people enter rooms. No one else enters a room like Chris Blackwell. It sometimes seemed he was there already when the room and its occupants materialized around him. "Wh'oppen?" his usual greeting.

Ten days before the arrival of Bob and Tosh outside the office door, Chris had set his briefcase on the table, popped it open, moved his spare pair of jeans and a sheaf of unused plane tickets aside, pulled out a white album sleeve, and explained he'd signed a band from Kingston. He asked me if I'd ever been to Jamaica. The question provoked a memory for me.

When Harry Belafonte's album *Calypso* came out, I was a pale eleven-year-old boy in a small town near the Illinois/Wisconsin border, trying to imagine a world other than the one where dour, serious children mimicked their dour, serious parents. I lived in the fork of a tree in the backyard where I stashed purloined cigarettes and paperbacks boosted from the rack by the door of the pharmacy. The tree provided a vantage point for watching the passage of clouds and kept the rest of my family from having to think about me. This satisfied them because they already had a great many things to think about. Matters I could not guess held their attention. As my tree would sway on the prairie wind, I used to hum the tune to

Jamaican Farewell and imagine myself as a sailor watching Kingston fade into the Caribbean behind me.

"Never been," I said.

"You'll have to go someday," Chris said.

He proceeded to tell us the history of the Wailers, which, by now, has become the fodder of dozens of books and video documentaries.

Stuck in London in winter when they came to Island, Chris gave them funds to go home to Jamaica and make an album. Others at Island figured Chris had thrown the money away. Today, it seems self-evident that *Catch A Fire* would become a platinum album, but it was the first album by a reggae performer released in the US. Occasional hit singles and compilation albums featured reggae and ska beats, but they were considered novelties. Few, if anyone, guessed album-buying FM listeners would be interested in a Jamaican band. Not only did Bob return with an album, but the album Bob brought back was stunning.

Chris Blackwell left us with the acetate and two concerns. He wasn't sure American audiences would handle the patois that might make the Wailers incomprehensible to non-Jamaicans. Also, these guys had a reputation of being difficult to work with. He added that Bob was in Delaware staying with his mother but he would be coming to New York and could stay in the Island suite at the Windsor Hotel.

XXXXXX

I couldn't imagine how we wound up with a master copy of an album the band hadn't even heard. I expressed astonishment. Bob said again that they hadn't heard it. With no alternative coming to mind, my inherent optimism kicked in and I suggested we move into the back room where I could put it on the turntable.

The smaller small room was windowless. The wall opposite the door was floor-to-ceiling shelving

NOT ONLY
DID BOB
RETURN
WITH AN
ALBUM,
BUT THE
ALBUM BOB
BROUGHT
BACK WAS
STUNNING.

for records, a reel-to-reel tape machine, and commensurate speakers, amplifier, and turntable. The system could have blown the stuffing out of the beanbag chairs in front of it.

Amid the beanbags, green glow lights floated on TV trays, a Seven-Up bottle offered its dancing green halo, and an endless blue wave rocked back and forth slowly above it all on top of the bookcase. These furnishings, completed by an assortment of London souvenir ashtrays, embarrassed me when I walked in with Bob and Tosh. From the red, white, and blue beanbags to the blue wave wobbling back and forth, the room seemed ironic and cute. But we were sitting

Tosh showed no discernable response, beyond a tightening in the region of his jaw I may have imagined. Two minutes into the track when Wayne Perkin's guitar took over for a forty-second solo, Tosh muttered something like, "Blow-clot, Bomba-clot, Ras-clot," the significance of which was becoming clear to me.

Bob had taken the tapes to London and worked with Chris Blackwell adding instruments. He was there when Wayne Perkins's guitar and Rabbit Bundrick's synthesizer filigree contributions were added. But Bob wouldn't have heard the final mix because Chris made further changes after Bob went home.

ALL I COULD FIGURE OUT WAS THAT THE ENERGY IN THE ROOM BECAME UNPREDICTABLE WEATHER.

down to listen to an album that began with four tracks: *Concrete Jungle*, *Slave Driver*, *400 Years*, and *Stop That Train* that, 45 years later, still deliver radical messages of stunning force, conspicuously devoid of irony.

The Wailers recorded *Concrete Jungle* in Jamaica with a thirty-two-second instrumental intro before the first lyric was sung. But when Bob brought it to the Basing Street studios in London, he and Chris Blackwell added instruments and remixed the sound of the album in search of a formula that dovetailed reggae with American rock and R&B tastes. In the version we were listening to, that thirty-two-second intro featured a strident clavinet, reflecting the energy Stevie Wonder brought to Superstition. A bass riff announces itself, followed by an unexpected hesitation, and then a crescendo of descending base notes seemingly in dramatic response, another pause, further exposition from the bass, now aided in discourse by the clavinet's pulse. As a barely discernable melody develops, it's paired with an improbable guitar that sounds nothing at all like Tosh's.

Bob's surprise, however, would not have compared to Tosh's. The first time Tosh heard the finished album he was sprawled on a beanbag beside me. A southern rock influenced guitar track could not have been what he expected to hear overlaid on his song *Concrete Jungle*. His own guitar had been pushed into the background along with his vocals.

On the one hand, Bob had to absorb additional changes that were made to the album and, on the other, he had to consider how all this would register with Tosh.

All I could figure out was that the energy in the room became unpredictable weather. I gave up and listened to the music, admiring Tosh's gravel baritone, like a train off the tracks, tearing through the landscape. I shook my head at the power of it. "Some, they live in big, but most live in small. They just can't find no food at all" he sang, and then, as if a kind of underlining of his own lyric, added, "I mean, starving."

117

"Rass-clat," he said next to me.

Tosh's long legs and plaid pants looked ridiculous sprouting out of a beanbag. I'm sure I looked equally far-fetched. I sported an impressive collection of narrow-shouldered suits with bellbottom pants. Some were seersucker.

Tosh took off his dark glasses in the dimly lit room, but as far as I could detect, there was little eye contact anywhere among us. When Side One ended, I turned the record over and we listened to Side Two. No words were spoken. The light danced around the 7-Up bottle.

The situation was altogether inadequate. The Wailers had performed together for a decade. Marley and Tosh were stars in Jamaica, intending to make a similar impact in America. And here they were, sitting in beanbags in a miniature office that wasn't even a proper record company office. DK and I were the closest thing Island Records had to a New York office, but we were responsible for Ackee Music, Inc., a music publishing company that administered US rights for Island Music's songwriters. We didn't have publishing rights to the Wailer's songs. Bob had signed those rights elsewhere.

On top of that, Island Records in the US was distributed by Capitol Records, and that arrangement was not in good shape. Chris had signed the deal when Artie Mogull ran Capitol, but Artie had been replaced and the new administration displayed the typical ambivalence toward projects whose success would reflect well on their predecessor.

In their place, I think I would have felt an ache of betrayal. Perhaps several betrayals.

They were like artists commissioned to create a mural who begin to realize their magnificent work has been painted on a stage prop for a fly-by-night carnival.

When the album finished, we moved back to the round table in the other room. I let the album play again, in the background at a lower volume.

I had a small antique toy, a four-inch figure of a man made of stamped tin with four propeller blades dangling from his bowler hat, that I kept on the table. A friend gave it to me. I think the friend thought it suited me. When you spun the rod that emerged from his bowler hat, the propellers rose to horizontal and rotated furiously, shaking the little man's body. The toy was too heavy to fly. No matter how fast the rod spun, he never left the tabletop. His optimism, however, was irresistible. He was like a three-legged dog, getting nowhere fast, but trembling at the chance.

XXXXXX

Despite Capitol's ambivalence, *Catch A Fire* was released to considerable fanfare. The first pressing was shipped in sleeves that replicated a Zippo lighter. When the lid was lifted on its grommet hinge, a cutout flame emerged in front of the album. Capitol Records declined to press the records using red vinyl, but the jacket looked great anyway.

What should have been the next step, a tour to support a major album release, barely happened at all. No agency was willing to book the Wailers. Their conspicuous affinity for marijuana could have been a problem. Of course, every other band touring America at the time participated in that habit, but other bands didn't elevate

WHAT SHOULD HAVE BEEN THE NEXT STEP, A TOUR TO SUPPORT A MAJOR ALBUM RELEASE, BARELY HAPPENED AT ALL.

ganja to the status of a religious icon.
Then, too, the Wailers had canceled a tour
in England. Stories circulated that they were
violent. Grainy black and white promotional
photographs of them tempted the viewer to look
for concealed weapons and did nothing to
discourage the stories.

Lee Jaffe, a filmmaker friend of Bob's, showed
up at the office, found a chair, a phone, and
went to work. Gradually, something vaguely
resembling a tour came
together. Venues were
offered but were available
only at times that made no
logistical sense. A customs
clearance issue meant the
band had to fly into Canada
and reenter at Niagara
Falls. Tosh smoked ganja
coming across the bridge.
He was somehow still allowed
in, but the customs officials
confiscated his pipe. He
complained extensively.

The first shows in Boston went
well. The following shows took
place at Max's Kansas City on
Park Avenue South in New York
City. Max's was already
legendary. A thick scarlet
laser beam from a building
across the avenue shot through Max's, all the
way to the restaurant in back. Rumor had it,
you would lose a hand if you passed it through
the light. That's why the beam was way up
there. The first floor of Max's had a high,
ornate ceiling and the beam passed through
billowing cigarette smoke.

To reach the performance space upstairs at
Max's, you climbed a long, narrow stairway.
Bands, roadies, and audiences arrived by
making that trek.

During the week of July 18, 1973, the Wailers
were booked with Bruce Springsteen and the
E-Street Band. The plan was for each band to

DURING THE WEEK OF JULY 18, 1973, THE WAILERS WERE BOOKED WITH BRUCE SPRINGSTEEN AND THE E-STREET BAND.

play three one-hour sets per night, with time
to turn over the audience in between. I imagine
Bruce and band didn't think much of playing
three interrupted sets each night, but I didn't
have to imagine what the Wailers thought about it.

Perhaps that week in July should have been a
seminal moment in popular American music. But
it was not the case. Neither band sounded great.
Swapping out equipment meant each brief set
suffered from a ragged start. Despite the number
of people who claim, retroactively, to have
been there, the room held a hundred people at
most and didn't sell out. Each band's audience
held little interest in the other band and
sometimes walked out.

At the end of The Wailer's first set, played before a tepid crowd with the commotion downstairs loud enough to compete with the music, we found ourselves stalled on the narrow stairs trying to figure out how to pass the time before the second set. Someone arranged a van to drive back to the Chelsea Hotel where the band was staying, although they'd have to turn back almost the moment they arrived.

The brothers in the band, Family Man and Carly Barrett, whose bass and drums created the heartbeat of the Wailers, decided to stay at Max's to check out the infamous restaurant downstairs.

I turned on the stairs to Bob and suggested we pass the time by driving around in my car, parked outside. Bob agreed. And so it happened that we climbed into a little green Toyota with a perpetually low right rear tire to wander up and down the Avenues.

Smoke billowed before we traveled a block. It curled across the window in front of me. Bob's ability to stay on topic under the influence astonished me.

We talked about intellectual property. It was of interest to both of us. I'd come to New York from Chicago in 1969 and worked my way into a position at ASCAP, the performing rights licensing organization. My job involved working with songwriters and publishers. My sympathies were with songwriters, but in my position, I'd been given the ability to see all angles of the industry and I loved to talk about it.

Bob's interest was more personal. Prior to signing with Island, the Wailers' records produced in Jamaica sold in England, but the band never got paid for them. The Jamaican version of licensing was a form of outright piracy with its own logic. As I came to understand it, songwriters in the Jamaican version bore roughly the same relationship to their songs as weavers would to their carpet. Once it is sold, the carpet's ownership has transferred. The record producer owned it and could do whatever he wanted with it.

As far as Bob was concerned, if that's how the game was played, he could work with it. After all, a weaver can make another carpet and could use the same pattern on that carpet if he wanted to do so. The weaver could sell the second carpet without worrying about the owner of the first carpet. In the same way, Bob figured a new recording should be a new transaction, even a recording of an old song.

We shared our frustrations with systems intended to compensate songwriters that wound up discouraging them instead—if not outright robbing them.

Bob asked what Ackee Music did for our share of sales. I explained that record companies made a habit of underpaying royalties. Often they assumed an unjustifiably high percentage of albums shipped would be returned. Our business was to be sure that we got our share. The work of the abacus.

We had factory work in common. I worked at an International Harvester plant on Chicago's West side in college. Bob worked at Dupont in Delaware while living with his Mom.

As the Toyota worked its way up Park Avenue to somewhere above 90th and then trundled back down Lexington, we talked and laughed. I saw Frank Barcelona, the head of Premier Talent, majestically parading up the boulevard in a long coat. I pointed him out to Bob. Premier had passed on the Wailers.

XXXXXX

By the time the Wailers played Max's, they already recorded a second album, *Burning*. The album had yet been released, but one of the songs from it, *Get Up, Stand Up*, was part of their live set. It was an anthem, a great closing song with its on-your-feet message and seemed destined to break through radio airplay. Written by Bob and Tosh in collaboration, the song provided insight into the way their thoughts both overlapped and did not. Their relationship at that point fluctuated between tenuous and

IN THE CONTROL ROOM, EACH FAILURE TRIGGERED RISING IMPATIENCE,

acrimonious. It seemed possible that the success of *Get Up, Stand Up* might help to glue the band together again.

One thing stood between *Get Up, Stand Up*, and airplay: the last verse of the song, which Tosh sang, challenged the Catholic Church, if not Christianity as a whole, dismissing it with the phrase "bullshit games."

I had to explain to Bob and Tosh that the word "bullshit" crossed the line. A record containing that word would be off the table. "And by 'table' I mean the 'turntable.' As in no airplay," I said, hoping to be amusing. I wasn't comfortable trying to convince them to rerecord a song, let alone change the words of it. But Island and Capitol wanted it.

As we sat at the round table in the office reflecting on the sensitivity of censors and expectations of record executives, two pigeons settled on the north-facing ledge outside the windows. With the vent windows open to let the smoke from Tosh's chalice and my cigarette escape, we could hear a soft cooing that sounded like courtship. A third pigeon arrived on the ledge of the East-facing window a moment later. This pigeon ruffled his neck feathers and began to pace, his head bobbing with impatience. He couldn't see the other two birds, whose courtship carried on unabated around the corner of the building.

Tosh said, "Whiteworst" softly. This was one of his names for Chris Blackwell. The remark caused a burst of collective laughter that propelled all three birds off the ledge.

We booked time at A&R Studios, and the Wailers went in to record a version of *Get Up* that radio stations could play. The song was already terrific. Superb. Ultimately, the BBC would name *Get Up, Stand Up* "the most important song of the twentieth century."

One word had to be replaced. It seemed straightforward. Pick a different word and sing it.

They recorded dozens of takes. Each time, Carly Barrett's rippling drum beat would fling the song into motion, Bob would sing his verses, and finally, three minutes into the song, Tosh would step to the microphone and file his contribution. Sometimes he said "bullshit games" again. Sometimes he would hum the line or be silent when the moment came. Sometimes he would contrive a substitute and then everything would stop long enough for those of us in the control booth to decide whether "shitstem" was going to pass. It wouldn't, even disguised to sound almost like "system."

In the control room, each failure triggered rising impatience, but on the other side of the glass, there was no sign of anxiety. More than

BUT ON THE OTHER SIDE OF THE GLASS, THERE WAS NO SIGN OF ANXIETY.

a few times we tried to suggest alternative phrases. The band sometimes debated things for a moment or two. But most of the time, everyone looked at everyone else and simply began again. There seemed a serene confidence that, somewhere along the line, Tosh would find a resolution. I didn't see a hint of annoyance among the band, so I followed their lead and focused on Family Man's bass. His command of the absent note held the authority of a Zen master. He could create a sonic lapse that would walk around your mind like a ghost.

Eventually, everyone in the control room wound up where the band was all along. It really didn't matter when or how the problem was solved. There wasn't anything better to do with the night than to listen to a great band perform a classic song again and again.

Then, just like that, Tosh sang: "I'm sick and tired of your ism-schism/getting down and go to heaven in Jesus' name/we know and we understand/the mighty God is a living man."

"Ism-schism!"

The song ended. The Wailers looked at the control booth. Everyone looked at everyone else. In the opera Turandot, when the princess's questions are posed to the stranger and he responds, a group of court stewards repeat the response while they search the records to decide if the response is correct. Were someone to turn the Wailers life into an opera, a similar scene could be written for this moment. "Ism-schism," "ism-schism," "ism-schism?" "I'm in," someone says. Others nod. We are there.

The musicians came into the control room, with the final version of *Get Up, Stand Up* pulsing out of the studio monitors. Smiles everywhere. It is a moment of unabashed celebration. When we come out of the studio, there's light in the East. Dawn just beyond the warehouses across the street.

Get Up, Stand Up didn't chart well, especially taking into consideration that it would come to be selected as the defining song of the century. In parts of the country, the first line Bob sang precluded airplay: "Preacher man don't tell me heaven is over the earth/I know you don't know what life is really worth."

XXXXXX

I push the button to disconnect from my call with Sam Sutherland at Billboard and immediately dial Bob.

"Yah."

"Hey Bob, it's Walt Schaefer. How're ya doin?"

"Yah, mon."

"We got some news about the single."

"Wha?"

"A friend of mine writes for Billboard. He says your single will be on the charts when they're released next week."

WAILERS IS BUBBLING UP UNDER ALL THE HOT 100 SONGS.

"Yah. That's good."

"It is good." I pause. "It's not actually on the Hot 100 singles, but they're going to put it at one-hundred six. That makes it one of ten singles they call bubbling under the Hot 100. We were hoping it would chart higher, but this is good."

"Wha? Wha? Wha? Wha? Wha?"

Pause. I definitely had Bob's attention. I interpreted his volley of questions as meaning he might not understand how Billboard's charts worked.

"They rank the top-selling hundred records for the week," I explained, "and then they list another ten songs they expect good things for. They say those ten are bubbling under."

"Ierie. Yah. So right now? We bubbling on the Hot 100?"

"Right." Hmmm. I realized I was in a jam. If Bob spread the word that the song was somehow on top of the popular music chart, it will be embarrassing for both of us when the issue hit the newsstands and the song wasn't even among the top hundred. "Well, no. The song is bubbling under. It's under the Hot 100." I didn't want to sound discouraging. "But that's good," I added.

"That's great, Yeah, man. That's great. The Wailers are bubbling on the Hot 100."

"Yeah. It's good Bob. But the song is bubbling under, not on, the Hot 100."

"Seen."

"So, yeah, another way of saying would be that the song is on the chart at number one-oh-six."

"Bubbling under."

"Right, bubbling underneath."

"Yeah, mon. Yeah. Truth. Wailers is bubbling up under all the Hot 100 songs. That's good, good news, mon."

"Okay, Bob. I get you." I paused to recalibrate. "Yeah, you could say that. Right. Sure. Bubbling under."

"Wailers bubble under all the others," Bob said. "Truth. Fire underneath make water boil. Wailers bubble under, just like the Mighty Dread. Just like Jah."

Bob won.

"Seen." I said. "You guys are bubbling under everything." I'm sure I even said, "every-ting" in my enthusiasm.

"Irie-ieghts!" he said.

"Irie!" I said.

At the end of this conversation, I thought we were in agreement that, while it was not accurate to describe either the song or the band as "bubbling on the Hot 100" it would be true in a metaphorical sense—which I came to understand that was how truth existed from Bob's perspective - to say that the Wailer's music was bubbling underneath the Hot 100.

XXXXXX

Sometime after *Catch A Fire* and *Burning* but before *Natty Dread* was released, Ackee Music HQ moved to Los Angeles. In retrospect, it was a dubious move for my career in the music industry. For a hundred bucks plus fuel, I hired a college student to drive the green Toyota from Manhattan to Los Angeles. Island Records purchased a rambling house on Sunset Boulevard and Ackee Music took over the upstairs. Same round white table, more room, more director chairs. DK, the abacus, and the little tin helicopter man in their customary places.

In the offices downstairs, a reconfigured Island Records began to take shape.

A charming, legendary promo-man was hired to assist Capitol's efforts and eventually take over the process. This was akin to hiring a drill sergeant to manage a modern dance collective.

The promo-man told me I couldn't drive around Los Angeles in a Toyota sedan. He had a friend who trafficked reconditioned Mercedes. I rented a place in Laurel Canyon and bought a huge convertible white Mercedes with leather seats. Ascending Laurel Canyon each evening, I watched the gas gauge needle descend.

Problems arose in the house on Sunset Boulevard. Bands from England become comfortable in the New York offices, so they came upstairs to see DK, to get another lesson on the abacus, or to spin the propellers of the little tin man. Tucked in their offices, Island Records officials didn't always know an Island artist was in the building.

Cocaine, that utterly harmless attitude adjuster, made inroads everywhere. For a while, everything looked good. And then, one day, you noticed the

IT WAS A MATTER OF TIME AND THEN IT WAS TIME.

consistent users were prone to grievous delusions. By the time we knew it wasn't harmless after all, we were left standing in the wreckage, staring at one another.

It was a matter of time and then it was time.

I resigned and turned over the Mercedes, was given a golden handshake, and hired as a consultant. Bob asked me to act as a consultant to his music publishing company, Tuff Gong Music, and I did that. But by this time, things were changing fast. Bob had new management and security and camp followers.

While I was in L.A., The Wailers played at the Hollywood Bowl. It was an important performance. Although they were aggregating fame worldwide, their success in America was only a little better than bubbling under. Our seats were amid the music industry section – the best seats in the house for classical music, no doubt, but the worst place to see a concert. The Bowl was sold out. Around the edges of the hall a dance party was unfolding, but in the fine seats up front, everyone sat. Finally, as a last encore, with the rest of the house going berserk, the band launched into *Get Up, Stand Up*. I stood and began dancing, but from behind me, came a loud whine, "Hey, fucking please, sit down!" ❿

MOROCCO AND MY FIRST EID KABIR

Words by Tiara Darnell

Tiara Darnell, a Maryland native, is a freelance writer, podcaster, and videographer based in Portland, Oregon. Her work has appeared in *Portland Monthly*, *Sprudge*, *Willamette Week*, and *Medium*, among other publications. She is currently the host and producer of *High, Good People* a "potcast" about the burgeoning cannabis industry from the perspective of people of color.

Tiara is a returned Peace Corps Morocco volunteer.

T

he road from Marrakech to Ouarzazate is known as "the gateway to the Sahara," a moniker enchanting as it is deceptive. Old Berbers call it "tchka," which means "tough road," and their description is more accurate.

It was late afternoon when I left Marrakech. The olive and date trees bid bslaama! as the city went from enormous sprawling metropolis to a speck on the horizon. The elevation crept, then came the s-curves and switchbacks. Three hours and forty-five minutes of them climbing and descending through the Atlas Mountains, skinny roads with no room for guardrails, sometimes etched onto cliff-faced canyon walls. To keep motion sickness at bay, I focused on the awe-inspiring peaks and valleys, the hillsides dotted with content sheep, little streams where groups of women did laundry while laughing and gossiping with one another, and the cafés of sleepy one-road villages filled with Moroccan men drinking coffee and smoking cigarettes.

Around sunset, the trees ceased, and desert hills blushed in the soft light. The Atlas Mountains ended, and the Sahara began. This is where Ouarzazate, "the city without noise," is situated. It became my home for the next two years.

Some months later, early in my first-year volunteering with the U.S. Peace Corps, I hoped someone in the host community would invite me to their home for the Eid al-Kabir celebration, even though I wasn't Muslim or Moroccan, and despite my shaky command of darija (Moroccan Arabic). Eid al-Kabir honors the prophet

BEHIND THE KNIVES, THRIVING HIBISCUS AND JASMINE FLOWERS GREW STEADILY UP THE APARTMENT BUILDING'S WALLS.

Ibrahim, who was set to sacrifice his son, Ishmael, to demonstrate his commitment to God. Convinced of Ibrahim's devotion, God spared Ishmael and provided a ram to kill instead. Therefore, on this holiday, across the Muslim world, it is the tradition for families to slaughter a goat or sheep.

Serendipitously, I met a graduate of my alma mater who lived in Ouarzazate. His name was Khaled Al-Abbadi, a Yemeni-American Fulbright Scholar. When I mentioned I didn't have plans for Eid al-Kabir, Khaled invited me as a guest to celebrate, Yemeni-style, with his wife Fatima and their infant daughter. This Ramadan was special, said Khaled. He planned to personally slaughter a sheep for the first time.

The Al-Abbadi family lived in one of the nicer residential areas of Oz. They shared a small, gated courtyard with a Moroccan family that lived in the apartment below. When I entered the courtyard on the afternoon of Eid, the first thing I saw was a large sheep tethered to a pole. "Aww, snap! This is happening," I thought to myself as intrigue crept in. To the left on the stoop sat a set of knives, shining in the sun atop a clean white towel. The blades were

polished and sharp. Behind the knives, thriving hibiscus and jasmine flowers grew steadily up the apartment building's walls. But the odor of wet hay and fresh manure coming from the sheep dominated the scent of jasmine, reminding me of the animal's imminent fate.

Fatima came out to greet me. She kissed me on both cheeks. Khaled followed. We shook hands and exchanged pleasantries while touching our right hands to our hearts, a sign of respect in Muslim culture. Khaled was nervous about slaughtering the animal. He admitted the anxiety of it kept him up through most of the night. Dark circles lay under his eyes. He was worried about not efficiently ending the sheep. Fortunately, his downstairs neighbor, a butcher, was there to help guide him through the process.

The call sounded from nearby minarets, and Fatima and Khaled went to mid-day prayers. After they finished, they returned to the courtyard and Fatima lit incense. The perfumed smoke wafted all around us. It was silent as Khlaed and his neighbor prepared the sheep, bounding and pinning it against the mosaic tiles decorating the courtyard floor. Once secure, Khaled offered a prayer thanking God

HIND THE KNIVES, THRIVING HIBISCUS   BEHIN
JASMINE FLOWERS GREW STEADILY   AND J
THE APARTMENT BUILDING'S WALLS.   UP THE

for the health and blessings of his family, and the food that the soon-to-be sacrificed sheep provided. Then, in what seemed like one fluid motion, he reached for the largest of the knives, positioned himself over the sheep, and slit its throat.

I expected to be shocked and to feel disgusted in that moment, but I wasn't. I was lost in thought seeing where our meal would come from. I couldn't tear my eyes away from the bloody scene, but when I finally did my first glance was down at my right sleeve. I wore a white shirt because white symbolizes peace, but at that moment all I could think was, "Why the hell did I wear white to a sheep slaughter!?" Apparently, Khaled didn't fully clear one of the main arteries, so blood spurted and sprayed instead of draining cleanly. The butcher, watching keenly from behind Khaled, muttered something I couldn't understand, and Khaled reacted quickly to rectify the mistake. We all watched on in silence as the sheep's hooves scraped the ground as it contorted under Khaled's grip for a few moments. Its writhing slowed as it bled out, and soon the sheep was completely still.

It was then that the butcher stepped in, and with help from Khaled, strung the sheep up to finish draining. Afterward, he blew air through the sheep's anus. I asked why he was doing that, and I understood that it helped to separate the skin from the flesh, so he could skin it properly. Khaled said he planned to preserve the sheep's hide so he could use it as a prayer rug.

In addition to fasting, charity is one of the five pillars of Islam, and it extends to sharing the bounty of Eid al-Kabir with others. After the sheep was butchered, Khaled gifted a large portion to the neighbors. Fatima again lit incense and began to skewer chunks of meat and heart (a treasured delicacy) wrapped in what looked like oily, white netting. It was sheep fat and it sizzled seductively over the blistering grates of the small charcoal grill. I asked if she wanted help cooking, but Fatima refused, insisting I relax and be a guest in her home. It wasn't hard to do but resisting the temptation to sneak a sample was. The meat smelled divine! My mouth watered listening to her list the other traditional Yemeni dishes she previously prepared upstairs as she turned the perfectly caramelized kabobs over the heat.

I was ravenous when Khaled said we were to spend time with the neighbors before our meal. They, too, were grilling meat from a sheep they slaughtered earlier. When the sun finally set, the fast ended. The neighbors served olives, salad with boiled eggs, orange Fanta, bread and oil, and more of the sheep heart wrapped in fat. I already stomached goat heart on one of my first nights in Morocco because I didn't

want to be rude to my hosts. And even though it smelled good, my American sensibilities wouldn't let me get over how unappetizing it was to eat. But this was a special occasion though, so I stuffed one skewer's worth of heart into a comically large piece of bread. I hoped just to get it over with, but also to get away with eating enough to make them believe I was full when I swore "shbet, shbet," meaning "I'm satisfied, I'm satisfied." Alhamdullah! It worked!

After the first meal at the neighbors, we all went upstairs. Everyone, including the neighbors. I regretted filling up on bread as soon as I laid eyes on the feast Fatima prepared. There were three different types of salads, more olives, two enormous platters holding spiced chicken and turmeric rice, and a homemade green chutney I still crave to this day. We sat on cushions around the platters of food and ate communally. Fatima's homemade bread was our utensils. There was much rejoice ending the fast, but a new appreciation for the food and the warm company of new friends is what I took away from my first Eid Al-Kabir. ⓫

"WHY THE HELL DID I WEAR WHITE TO A SHEEP SLAUGHTER!?"

GIFT DE THRIFT

Words by Bonnie Ilza Cisneros
Artwork by Susan Sage

Bonnie Ilza Cisneros is a fourth-generation educator in a line of South Texas schoolteachers. Recent highlights include: earning an MFA from Texas State University, becoming a member of the Macondo Writer's Workshop, and a recipient of a National Association for Latino Arts and Culture artist grant. Moonlighting as DJ Despeinada, she spins vinyl soundscapes of the borderlands. Her poems and essays appear in *Front Porch Journal*, *El Retorno*, *Chicana/Latina Studies*, and *El Placazo*. Her essay/autohistoria, *The Ana Files*, has landed in the forthcoming issue of *River Teeth Journal*. Bonnie performs at cultural events, cantinas, and cemeteries. Her energy orbits around two Tejanita daughters.

e know that the best thrift stores are filled to the brim with second-hand junk and treasures waiting to be plucked.

These places we frequent used to be dank and dim, smelled like a hundred years of dust and other people's funk trapped within.

But that was then, and now the modern thrift store is neat and clean. The fluorescent lights are bright.

How many hours have we spent thumbing through rack after rack after rack of our community's cast-offs?

Through jackets and blouses and pants, through dresses and scarves and bags, we scan and we scan and we scan for that certain *pop!* of color or that certain *feeeeel* of fabric or that *print* that catches our eye and won't let go.

Scan and scan and scan.

Pause. Stop. Pull a prospect off the rack.
Eyeball it. Fondle it.
Check the label. Debate the size.

Hold it up against you and sometimes, sometimes, Jackpot! Sigh and swoon!

Then...lo and behold, the tag is green! And we know what that means!
Half off today.

It's *so* yours, mama, it's meant to be,
so you take it off the hanger, and keep on looking.

But sometimes it's all wrong, and sometimes you can't find shit,
it's not your day, so you rehang it and chalk it up to displeasing
the Thrift Store Gods.

You like the sounds of hangers sliding on metal racks,
the sweet tunes of '70's soft rock piped in, the *señora* next to you scolding her kid, the rumble of hands digging through so much stuff.

We are a society of so much stuff.

Me?

I know my eyes were trained to *see* by my mother who learned to stretch
minimum wage dollars to house and feed and clothe her daughters.

My ma learned early on that *ropa usadas*, thrift stores, garage sales, *pulgas* were the
places to score and make little girls' hearts soar:

a calico rabbit fur coat for that touch of 2nd grade winter's glamour,
a pink n' white gingham swimsuit that was retro before "retro" was in,
a genuine Cher doll with real eyelashes that outglammed the latest Barbie.

My mother taught us to find treasure in the trash, the divine in the dumpster,
she showed us how to dig deeper and look closer,
not only 'cause it's cheaper, but because it's worth more when you rediscover it,

it's a thrill to uncover it:

A Japanese teacup from 3,000 miles away,
A 1940's glass ashtray that Joan Crawford *just might* have thrown at one of her
lovers,
A string of love beads from some hippie's heyday,
A rhinestone pin letter "B" for Bonnie,
A green silk fringe shawl like Zelda Fitzgerald on a good day,
A clamshell clutch for your little-old-lady phase
A pair of maroon leather *botines* for when it's cold and you need to walk away.

My mom has the knack for finding treasure in unexpected places,
She can see what others pass over, See past years of neglect,
dusts stuff off, makes it shine.

And in doing so, she presents us with the world.

And, oh, the books we read!
And, oh, the records we heard!
And, oh, the movies we watched!

My mother taught us to remember and to learn,
in her pocket a library card
and a couple bucks,
enough to keep us entertained and educated.

She taught us that
all this stuff we make
and sew
and buy
and sell
and toss
and trade,
all these stories we re-tell
and clothes we re-sell,
help us remember we are revolving
around the same splendid sun
and we are spinning 'round together
and we make the world go 'round.

We know how to make do.
We know how to choose
our armor,
our costume,
our uniform,
and we crown ourselves with artifacts
and we are continuations from the past.

We know how long polyester really lasts,
we know that wool gets moth-eaten
and rhinestones tarnish,
and silk loses its sheen,
taffeta fades,
velvet crushes,
and denim frays.

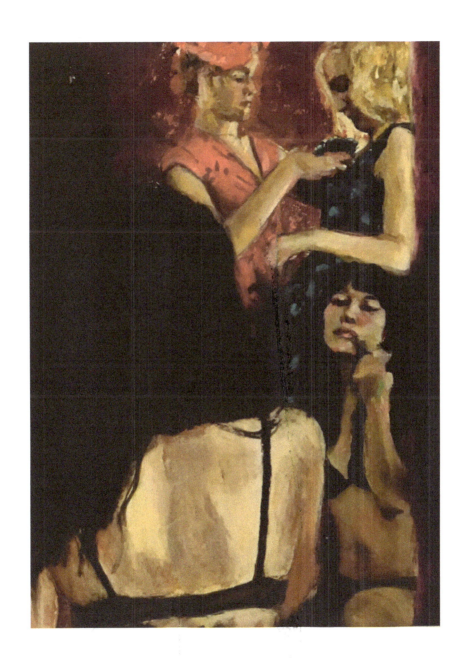

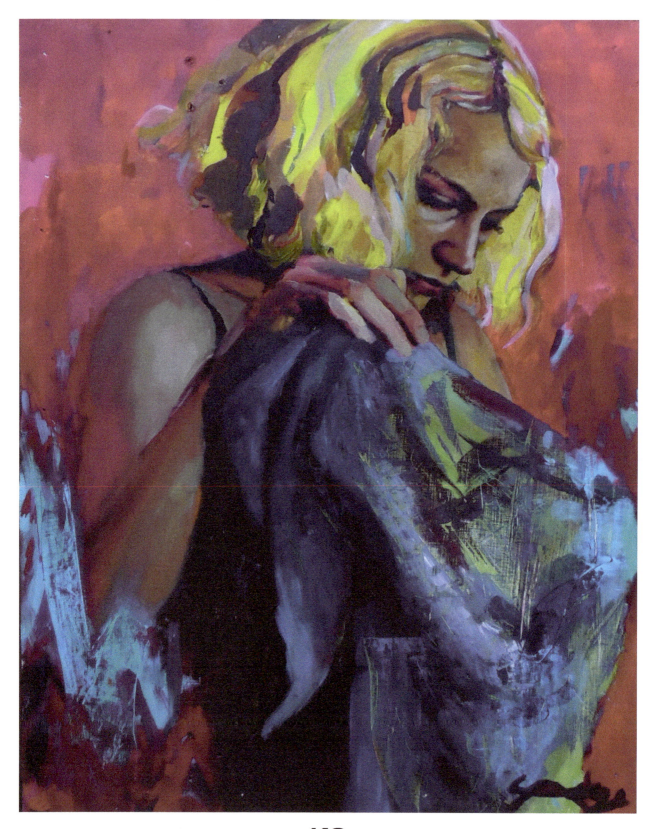

Yet we brush off the dust and
find what no one else can find,
we make do and
make ourselves up
for we are today
and that is the same as yesterday.

We are today
and we are the same as yesterday.

And maybe, after we're gone
and the stuff still remains,
some new eyes
will pick through our piles
and pluck out the swag
in our stacks of lost treasures
and sigh,
Oh, that is the one I've been looking for.🅑

SELF-MADE WOMAN

Finally, the big day arrived, and I boarded China Air for my flight to Bangkok. It was a weird flight path, flying over Canada with a stop in Anchorage, on to Taipei, and then to Thailand. The stopover in Anchorage was surreal. Winter had already set in as we landed in a snowstorm, and even though it was only 4 p.m., outside it was already pitch black. Having a two-hour layover, I deplaned to walk around the terminal. I was struck by how modern the airport was, but what really caught my eye were a pair of stuffed bears, a Kodiak grizzly and a Polar bear opposite one another, both standing tall. I was awed by the immense size of these beautiful creatures, their giant claws, teeth, powerful legs, thick fur, sharp eyes, and large black noses. How efficient these animals must be in the wild, I thought, saddened to find them dead inside this airport.

It could've been the impression those bears made on me, or the excitement of my pending surgery once I arrived in Bangkok, that brought on an overwhelming desire to call my mother. Whatever possessed me to do this I don't know, but by the time I realized it was a mistake, it was too late. She had answered the phone. I immediately felt uncomfortable—why did I call her? I started off with small talk, gradually telling her I was in Anchorage, on my way to Bangkok, Thailand. We'd had a few previous phone discussions about my upcoming gender change, none of which ever went well. Maybe, my thinking went, once she understood I was actually going through with sex reassignment surgery—that her son was on the cusp of fulfilling a lifelong dream to become a woman—there would be some loving support. Exactly the opposite happened. I'd played this badly and my mother pleaded with me on the phone not to go through with this and "hurt myself."

Words by Denise Chanterelle Dubois
Artwork by Stephanie Hatch

Denise Chanterelle Dubois is an actress, environmentalist, and businesswoman. She lives in Portland, Oregon. The following is from her memoir *Self-Made Woman* (The University of Wisconsin Press, ISBN 978-0-299-31390-6).

Soon the discussion revolved around those three words. Don't hurt yourself. I listened in stunned silence, angry at her for not supporting me in something that she had hints of my whole life and was in complete denial about. On top of hurt and rejection, I felt momentarily guilty over what I'd planned all these years. I was 49, recently divorced, broke financially, and a recovering addict. Two tragedies in my life, an abusive father and an addiction to crystal meth, had ironically turned out to help push me, giving me the resilience to take this step. My mother still didn't understand. The call ended with the two of us as far apart as ever.

There in the terminal, I stopped again at the Kodiak and the Polar bears. Nothing was going to take me away from who I really was inside. I returned to the gate and got back on that plane, free of doubt about becoming Denise.

It was sweltering in Bangkok, a heat not unlike the weather one Sunday afternoon decades earlier when my journey began, in the summer of 1958. I was 4 years old. My parents, sister, and I were on our way to the lake cottage owned by my grandparents. I can remember how huge the backseat of my parents' car seemed to me at that age. I saw the big shift handle on the steering column, smelled the musty car seats, and played with the window handle. My mother smoked a cigarette, my father a cigar. The telephone poles flew by. I counted the wires, watching them twirl and twist as we zoomed along the empty rural highway. If I lost count I started over again. I was very excited that we were going out to the cottage again because it meant I could play on the little dock and look out at the lake. I loved that lake. I could see all the way across it and look at the wind-capped waves blowing, the fishing boats

with people oaring, and the occasional outboard motor boat that always left a wake in the water. I liked watching the dancing dragonflies buzzing around and landing on the dock, where I'd try to catch them with no luck. I breathed in the scent of the fresh lake water and observed the sunshine reflect on the water and the small waves lap on the shore. I loved, too, the small yard that led to the lake, with its wispy willow trees, where the branches snapped like whips in the wind, and where Busha, my grandmother, had many Italian plum trees growing whose fruit I loved to eat. My earliest memory is of being under the kitchen table of our first house, in Milwaukee, eating a piece of bread with plum jam on it. I ate the whole thing and crawled out from under the table and asked my mother and aunt for another piece. They laughed and gave me one. In the yard, at the lake cottage, I was always on the lookout for that familiar shade of purple when those plums started to ripen.

Summer gatherings at the cottage meant plenty of alcohol being served, card playing, and Polish food—cold blood soup, kapusta, pirogues, cooked beets, mock chicken legs, raw hamburger with onions—all piled on platters set on a long table. Adults engaged in constant drinking and card playing, while pretty much ignoring what the kids were up to. That particular day my sister and I played on the dock without supervision. I hadn't learned how to swim yet, I was too young. As much as I liked the dock, I was afraid, too. The water looked so deep, dark, and forbidding between the wooden planks. I remember sitting down on the edge, next to a tied up small boat, and feeling the hot planks on the back side of my upper thighs as my tiny legs dangled over the water. My sister, only 19 months older than me but much taller, had climbed down into the boat. She was urging me

THE CALL ENDED WITH THE TWO OF US AS FAR APART AS EVER.

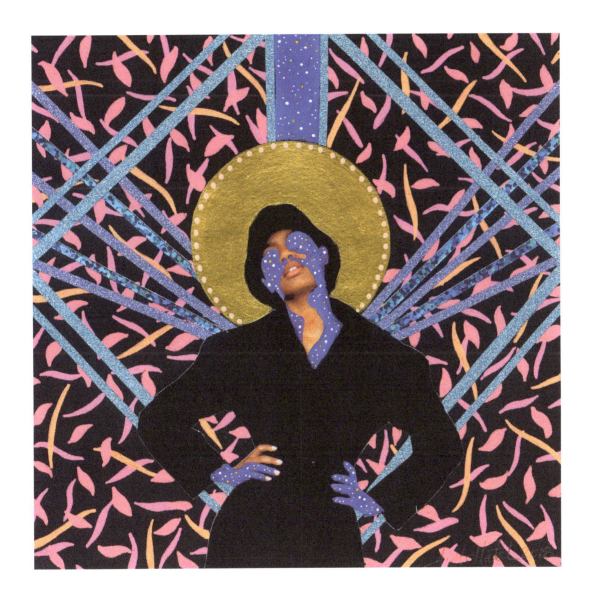

to do the same. I feared the worst. I had a premonition of falling in and drowning, but eventually she coaxed me into complying. I put my hands on the edge of the dock and tried to stretch my legs down to the boat. I was shaking; my legs were too short to make it. All I could do was get one foot on the edge of it, and when I released my grip of the dock, the boat pushed away.

I went into the lake like a thirty-pound bag of cement. I was about to drown, to die. In fact, I was about to be reborn.

In Bangkok I met with Dr. Chettawut the next morning to go over the plan, which would start unfolding later in the day with pre-surgery prep work. I was struck at how young the doctor was and impressed by his extensive knowledge about SRS. He had an engaging manner, spoke proficient English, and patiently answered all my questions, as well as reviewing my paperwork, which included a letter of recommendation from a psychiatrist, who happened to be the mother of one of my roommate's back in New York. She had been thorough, asking many questions about my life and how my RLE and HRT had gone. RLE and HRT are two crucial stages for anyone seeking gender reassignment surgery. The first, which stands for real-life experience, demanded that I live fully as a woman for one year. The second, hormone replacement therapy, added medications to the process.

Dr. Chettawut was satisfied. "You make a good candidate for this surgery," he said. I did have to sign off, however, in case something went wrong while I was under. The entire operation was expected to take about six hours. This was no simple procedure, I knew, and I was entrusting myself to Dr. Chettawut's skill. I also had to pay in full at this time, and since he didn't take checks, I handed over the large sum of

I WAS ABOUT TO DROWN, TO DIE. IN FACT, I WAS ABOUT TO BE REBORN.

cash I'd brought with me. The transaction felt odd as I watched the doctor's wife count the bills, something she was quite good at, I noticed.

With time to kill before being admitted to the hospital, I visited a shopping mall located next to my hotel. This was a part of the Bangkok I didn't see when I passed through the city many years earlier. The mall was enormous, sleek and sexy. The stores were like what you'd see in the U.S., but even more stylish and attractive. I wandered into a salon that offered mani-pedis, had one done, and then decided to have my hair trimmed and styled. When the attractive stylist handed me a mirror to view the results, I was dismayed by how short my hair was. The last thing I wanted on the eve of a sex change was hair that looked gender-neutral! I had spent two years growing my blonde hair out, and in just one hour it was back to practically square one. Pretending to like it, I sulked out of there self-conscious about my appearance. Back in my hotel room, I packed and then went down to wait in the lobby for my ride to the hospital from Dr.Chettawut's wife.

During the drive I refocused on what mattered. This is it, I thought, as we rode along hectic streets, passing areas of the city I remembered from a different time, a different life. Arriving at the hospital, I was struck by how ultra-modern it looked from the outside, even more so than many U.S. hospitals. We didn't bother to use the front entrance for the usual check-in processing. Dr. Chettawut had a revolving account here, his wife explained, so we entered via a side door and I was taken directly up to my room. It was spacious and bright, with huge windows that gave a view of the skyscrapers of downtown. My bed had an inflatable, alternating pressure mattress to help prevent pressure sores during my recovery, during which I'd be on my back, knees up, for five days straight. This was absolutely necessary to allow for proper healing. The room was private—no sharing with another patient—and there was access to English books and magazines. I noticed a big screen TV and thought how handy it would be in the coming days of bed confinement.

As Dr. Chettawut's wife prepared to leave, I asked her how the hospital staff even knew I was here since we had yet to even see an RN. She smiled, told me to relax, and assured me that the staff knew I was here, and then she was gone. I poked around my room, checked out the bathroom, and turned on the TV. There was cable and plenty of U.S. channels. I propped up my pillows and was watching a rerun of The Beverley Hillbillies when in walked two of the hottest nurses I'd ever seen. I mean they were so hot I had to ask them if they were actual nurses, which they confirmed in broken, giggling English. Their uniforms were exactly like what I'd seen in porn magazines. Next came the best part; they were here to shave my pubic hair! I could not believe these gorgeous nurses were here to do this "chore." I eagerly spread my legs, and they lifted my hospital gown. One of them said, "Oh, cute panties." That did it. Despite the Androcur, a female hormone, I was taking, I felt my penis growing hard. I laughed. It was like a final curtain call for the last hours of life as a man. The nurses were super-delicate with me, using a straight-edge sterile blade, and laughed at my half-erect penis, cluing me in that they'd seen this all before.

More nurses visited, taking my blood pressure, temperature, and chatting with me, always

IT WAS LIKE A FINAL CURTAIN CALL FOR THE LAST HOURS OF LIFE AS A MAN.

smiling, all beautiful and young. I couldn't help but compare them to what we had in the U.S. Well, there was no comparison. Thailand was just a younger country population-wise and it showed in the staff at this hospital. Later, I couldn't sleep and mentioned it. In minutes another hottie appeared to administer a shot in my ass. I awoke the next morning a bit disoriented, but the beauty pageant began again, and I was fine. Dr. Chettawut showed up for a final pre-op discussion. He asked me if I had changed my mind. "Nope, not at all," I replied. And with that confirmation it was all systems go. I was transferred to an operating bed and moved into the pre-op room for my general anesthesia prep work. In my final moments of consciousness, having been given a relaxant via an IV and feeling loopy, I jokingly instructed the staff to make sure they used enough stuff to put me under, even as I resolved to resist falling asleep. The last thing I remembered was looking up at the white ceiling in this cold room and seeing a giant green gecko just sitting there. How did that gecko get in here I wondered, and then nothing, complete darkness.

I was drowning in the deep, dark depths of the lake. I remember going straight to the bottom, screaming and struggling. My eyes remained open and I saw bubbles and green lake water surrounding me. I remember choking and gasping. Then suddenly I could breathe—I could breathe underwater. Out of nowhere, a green tornado had

AT MOMENT I WAS
E DRESS SHOULD
RT OF ME. THAT
SS FELT ELECTRIC.

I KNEW AT THAT MOMENT
A GIRL AND THE DRESS S
ALWAYS BE PART OF ME. T
SUMMER DRESS FELT ELE

WAS
ULD
AT
RIC.

I KNEW AT THAT MOMENT I WAS A GIRL AND THE DRESS SHOULD ALWAYS BE PART OF ME. THAT SUMMER DRESS FELT ELECTRIC.

I KNEW
A GIR
ALWA
SUM

begun to form and swirl around me. I blinked my eyes in amazement, as this green tornado kept moving around me. There was an air pocket between the water and myself. I remained very scared but somehow sensed that everything would be okay.

I heard people screaming up above. I wasn't paying attention to them, however, I was fascinated with this green tornado, thinking I should just go with this neat phenomenon and forget about what the muffled distressed sounds above were all about. Then I heard my mother yelling, telling me to put my arms up. Seconds later I was on the pier like a beached baby seal. My mother had grabbed my arms and yanked me out of the water. At least that's what I believe happened. The other version is that my father jumped in after he removed his wallet from his trousers and saved me. But I don't recall my father on the dock.

I lay on the dock soaking wet, spitting up water. Everyone was making a huge commotion about what had just happened. Then it happened. I was whisked—snuggled up in my mother's arms

while being framed and almost coddled by those beautiful plum trees—toward the cottage. Anyone still drinking and playing cards would've surely interrupted their game when I came through there, probably still coughing, or even crying. I was brought into a dim bedroom and laid down. My wet clothes were removed and taken away and put in the dryer. Meanwhile, I couldn't just lay there naked; that would not be right. So, I was clothed in the only child's garment readily available. I was put in a girl's dress. That was it—the transformative earthquake.

I must've been left alone to rest. The adults would've wanted to resume their drinking and cards, the kids their own games. How I loved the way that dress felt, how it looked on me with its ruffled shoulders, how the breeze blew underneath it, how it swirled about as I spun myself around. I knew at that moment I was a girl and the dress should always be part of me. That summer dress felt electric.

Gender roles were very strict in the Polish Catholic community I was raised in. I remember always wanting to be with the women at family gatherings like this one. Sometimes I would not be noticed and listened to their conversation, learning about things every young girl has the opportunity to find out about at that age. But sooner or later I was always forced back to the poker table, to the men with their liquor, cigars, and cigarettes. Nearly drowning had opened a new world for me, but in this cultural environment, it couldn't last. What happened next was predictable. Once my regular boy clothes had dried I was told to put them on. I became very upset, saying I didn't want to wear those anymore because they were boy clothes and I was a girl now. My father, plied with shots of whiskey, was furious. His angry stare told me that I was not going to win this duel, and reluctantly I did as I was ordered. I knew my mother wouldn't intercede on my behalf. She was a young woman and was most likely pretty drunk too.

My father and mother displayed no tolerance toward me wanting to be a girl. Their attitude didn't undo anything. My feminine side was born that day and alive inside me.

I WANTED TO JUMP OFF THE BED INTO THE AIR, DO A SOMERSAULT, AND RUN DOWN THE HALL YELLING THE WORDS, I AM A WOMAN NOW!

In my hospital bed on the November morning after my surgery, I slowly moved my arm, letting my hand creep down across my stomach towards the ultimate objective. A big smile spread across my face as my hand gently moved around the smooth, bandaged mound between my legs. I finally had my vagina. Tears of joy ran down my cheeks. From that day on Busha and Jaja's dock at the lake cottage in southern Wisconsin to the exotic city of Bangkok, my quest, my right, my destiny had come to pass. I wanted to jump off the bed into the air, do a somersault, and run down the hall yelling the words, I am a woman now! I could feel and sense a new life opening before me. At the same time there was much in my past that would not be transformed, that would keep trying to drown me if I let it. This is the hard truth and the

MAYBE THAT'S WHAT DREW ME HERE, TO BE CLOSE TO THE DARK WATER OF MY PAST

core of my story in the struggle to become Denise. Eventually, I would find a place of beauty and inspiration to write down the often painful events of my life, to examine behaviors that were self-destructive, delusional, even illegal. Fifty years of battles—inner and outer. That nurturing place turned out to be in Hawaii. On the island of Kauai, I live in an area of coastline with treacherous currents, whose name in the Hawaiian language means unfriendly water. Maybe that's what drew me here, to be close to the dark water of my past, waters that tried to drown me many times. I was saved once by the green tornado in the lake. To survive what came later, though, I would have to rescue myself. **B**

CHECKING OUT

Words by Craig Foster
Illustration by Wooden Cyclops

hoa! There's a little mold
on one of your strawberries,
my brother.

Dr. Fleming's smoothie.

You want a whole new basket?
I can get it for you. Or I can
just go grab one good berry
if you like this basket best.

Bait and switch.

I'm gonna get the berry. Just realized
we'll have to compost the rest of what
you've got there if we swap it all out.

Planet Earthworm.

I mean, the others look good. Except for
maybe this guy snuggling with the first
guy. I'll snag two new ones.

Remus and Romulus.

Chai can work on ringing you up while
I'm gone. Chai, man, can you key me out
and punch in your code for the rest of
the sale?

Tea for two, and two for tea.

Chai, dude. Stuff gets messed up at
closing otherwise.

It's not me, it's you.

OK. Right on, never mind. It's all
groovy. What if I take out the two bad
berries and sell you the basket for
half price. Cool?

Ice Station Zero.

Hey, thanks for your patience, people.
You guys are so awesome. We had a
little problem but it's getting fixed.
Chai can take you over on 3.

Three-card monte.

Chai-ho, yo, the far-out brother
in the suit should be next.

Monkey business.

You know what? I'm just gonna give
you these berries. This never should
have happened.

Instant karma.

Let me quickly fill out a stock keeping
slip so our people know the deal.
Just. A. Sec.

Form-fitting nits.

There's a righteous system that lets
this happen. We want you here, man.

The perfect mousetrap.

No bag today? Definitely totally
cool. I'll give you one of ours
so you can split.

Sack race.

I'm putting the berries on top
of the toilet paper.

Sundae, bloody sundae.

Thanks for keeping on. Gotta get it
right, right? Enjoy and maintain, brother.

Bread and circuses. ●

THE CONSORT

Words by Merridawn Duckler
Photography by Jamila Clarke

Merridawn Duckler is a writer from
Portland, Oregon and the author
of *INTERSTATE*, forthcoming from
Dancing Girl Press. Her fiction has
appeared in *Carolina Quarterly*,
Main Street Rag, *Green Mountains
Review*, with recent work in
Airgonaut, *Medusa's Laugh Press*
and *The Southampton Review*.
She was a finalist for the Sozopol
Fiction Fellowship and named
to the Wigleaf 50. Residencies/
fellowships include Yaddo, Squaw
Valley, SLS in St. Petersburg,
Russia, NEA, Vermont Post
Graduate Conference. She's
an editor at *Narrative* and the
international philosophy journal
Evental Aesthetics.

e are waiting to go on stage.

The venue is grand and today is my birthday. I don't feel ninety, let me tell you. Well, when I stand up too fast. The light man gives us a nod. That sounds wrong—is it light man? Anyway, he'll dim the house and we'll walk out: Walt who's been by my side forever, Reg, our most recent drummer, Ash, who is twenty-nine and last of all, me. Ash has my reeds and my pills. They're like airplanes. Who knows how those things get into the sky and who knows how some pellet changes your heart from bad to good. Told Doc I didn't want to take them and he said, "David, you've needed these for twenty years, you don't take them, and you die, then I killed the great David Becker. How's that going to sit with my retirement?" So, I did it for him, and let me tell you I don't do stuff for just anyone.

Ash has the playlist. Printed out nice and big. I could go off list tonight. It would surprise no one.

Good crowd out there. Good vibe coming from the seats. They may be waiting for me to fail or wondering how I look at ninety. Most of my life has been walking onto a stage. Out of ninety years, I've been playing the saxophone for seventy-five. I was king of it all when I believed I'd reached the end. Draw whatever conclusions you like, Ash's girlfriend taught me IDGAF. I said: Put in a comma and could be a cord progression: I, DGAF. She said: You're cute. Some things haven't changed in ninety years. Women been saying that to me all my life. Never handsome, but cute. As for women, which I have had plenty, there was only one: Ressie. She died in '96. I woke up that morning and the light was different. Couldn't put a

THAT'S NOT PASSION. THAT'S BREATHING.

finger on it. Heard a couple of days later from her sister. They wanted "Sunrise for Billy" for the service. I said sure. I don't license those things anyway. I got a guy for that.

I glance at Ash in jeans, sweater with a round neck, sneakers. Not that I can complain: I'm not even sure what I'm wearing. My wife, Jenny, dresses me. She's half-Islander. Buys me these too-large shirts, sets up photo shoots, and gets freebies and whatnot. Great cook.

The interviewers always want to know if playing is my passion. They always ask that same moronic question. I learned it was best to say yes, but it's not a question that makes sense to me. I been playing the saxophone for three-quarters of a century. That's not passion. That's breathing. They like to hear how I got my sax from Lester. Not exactly true, but that's another thing I've figured out: an idea repeated hardens into a fact. I was born in 1927 in Plymouth, Ohio. No recollection of any so-called childhood. My dad was a drunk who went out for a pack of cigarettes in '32 and never came back. My mom was also a drunk and I was raised by my grandmother,

Granny Lee, a strict old lady. Fourteen I was on my own. I used to set pins at the bowling alley and that's where I heard my first jazz. They had a little trio in the bar inside the alley and I would make a few quarters by running errands: buy smokes, put a note on the race, stuff like that. There was a guitarist, Tony Middle. He taught me a few chords. Said it would help with the ladies. I practiced in an alley and someone threw a bottle at me off the six-floor walk-up. Freak accident—it broke, bounced, and tore my thumb half off. Never healed right. So that was goodbye to the guitar. Another guy in the band gave me a sax out of pity. More in the mouth than the hands, he said, and that was that.

I did get one from Lester, but that was later.

I've played all over the world. Berlin, Paris, been to Japan more times than I can count. Argentina. Did a set in Buckingham Palace for the royals. Cold as hell and every kind of bottle out but no food. Didn't realize we were supposed to ask those guys in white gloves for anything we wanted to eat. Brits don't lay out a buffet, at least they didn't then. God, we were smashed during that set! Played in Israel. Most intense audience of my career. I tell the Buckingham story but don't really remember it. Those stories are like putting the needle down

Usually, that means one thing: high. Lost a lot of good players to various substances. You'd see those pinprick pupils and think: Oh, shit. I'm no saint but my heart arrhythmia was diagnosed early on. That's how I met Doc, in the emergency room, him sitting on the chair, pack of smokes visible in his left pocket.

Doc: What is your occupation, Mr. Becker?

Me: I play the saxophone.

Doc: Would you like to live or die?

Me: Uh, I guess live.

Doc: Your heart is weak. Stay off the stuff and live. Get on and die.

Me: You don't exactly mince words.

Doc: Not my job.

And here I am, ninety.

WHO SITS LIKE THAT AT THE PIANO?

on a record—the parts just start to play. But memory is a funny thing. Sometimes a small club, not at all famous, will appear to me so vividly, I can smell the smoke, taste the light, hear all the progressions as if they were being written in the air.

I didn't like Ash in the beginning. Walt and I had heard about him, of course. Jazz is a small world. Fits in your palm. I'd lost my keyboard player. Or maybe someone sent us. I don't exactly remember. No trio had picked Ash up.

Ash is looking down. He has a habit of staring at something no one else sees. Occurs to me right this minute that his eyes rest about keyboard height. Should tell him that after this gig. Kid, you are always looking at the board. He appreciates that kind of observation. I don't remember what he played that first time. I only remember how he sat. Like a guy waiting for a bus. One foot on the ground and his ankle crossed over the other knee while he played. Ticked me off. I used to have a temper—I guess I still do. Jenny got me these tapes.

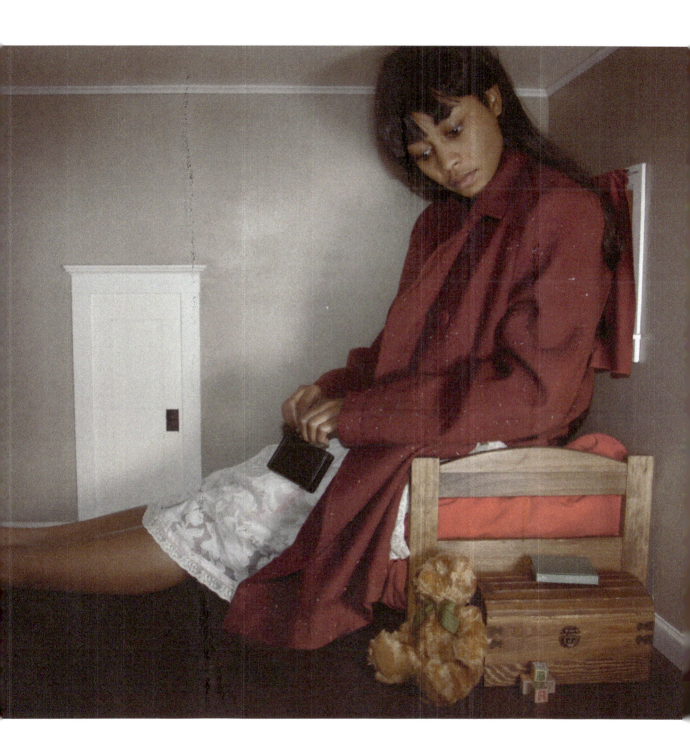

They don't help but when I play them she leaves me alone. In a rage, it comes back to me, the feeling of being finished, washed up. I try it out to see if it still has any power. But now all I can remember is how that stance drove me nuts, insouciant, bordering on disrespectful. Who sits like that at the piano?

We hired Ash, of course. Fantastic musician, crazy legs and all. I figured we'd get a year out of him. That was over a decade ago. In between we recorded "Fade Out" and seven Grammy's later, here we are. He does a lot of experimental stuff. Very prolific when we're not on tour. People assume I don't like anything modern, but they're wrong. Understand me: we are music-making creatures. That should blow your mind. It does mine. Animals make music, but they can't help it. Whereas we control what comes out, we decide. People don't understand the power of that. I'm not a religious guy. Sometimes people expect me to be, at ninety. Like they'll ask what are my plans. My plan is to play until the minute before there is nothing. I been the luckiest of men and the worst of humans. I have no thought in my head that I will see Ressie in some café in the sky.

She was nineteen. I have seen girls more beautiful but none that shone like that—from her skin to her smile. Her touch was just electric, and I could not get enough of it. We got married right away. She was like me, on her own. Worked as a typist but she would stay up until I came in at all hours. I can still see her, hair fluffed over the covers.

HER TOUCH WAS JUST ELECTRIC, AND I COULD NOT GET ENOUGH OF IT.

Dawn rising on angels was how it looked to me. Year two, Ressie got pregnant. I didn't know how I felt about that but it wasn't like today when you tell everyone the minute you have any kind of feeling of even the most minimal sort. I kept my reservations to myself. Ressie was over the moon. We didn't have any money, but then we didn't know anyone who did.

I was on tour when Ressie called the club. I think it was in Atlanta. I knew right away something was wrong. Just the feel of the receiver in my hand was cold. She said, "Now I gotta give birth and it's not like we planned." I told her she was gonna be fine. Said we were young and strong and the future was full of hope. "I just need you to come and hold my hand." I said yes. I finished the set and we got on the bus for Mississippi. We played two nights in Kansas City. Had a two-week stand in Chicago. Somewhere in some godforsaken hole in Ohio, place with one of those nets up because they throw bottles at you, I got a note. It said: They buried him on Tuesday. I named him Billy, after my uncle.

I have no excuses. I was sober, I knew what I was doing. I got my punishment, which was no more Ressie. I only remember looking out the window of the bus, at the houses going by, and I thought I shouldn't be like my old man who skipped. I should finish the tour. Never a day I don't regret my actions but the worse truth, if I'm being truthful, is that if I had it to do all over again, I would do exactly the same.

Ash moves his weight from foot to foot. We got about two minutes before curtain rises.

When we were recording "Fade Out" which, by the way, was an effect the Beatles invented, we knew we had something special, even though it almost didn't get made at all. It changed our lives with nicer cars, better cigars, autographs that became tattoos. On the road, better bus, bigger rooms. Walt has been with me since day one, otherwise a rotating crew. Finally, I did ask him, Kid, why do you sit like that at the piano? You look like a moron. He said: My mom took in sewing and that's how she sat at the sewing machine. Vietnamese sit differently than me and you. I said: You're Vietnamese? He said: The half of me that sits. He's full of surprises, that one.

x x x x x x x x x x x x

Magazines want to know how I relax before a big show. I got a stock answer for that one, too, though I forget it sometimes now. Probably that breathing thing Jenny taught me. But what I really do to relax is I think about practicing. Just in my room, hours and hours, practicing. Up and down, in and out, letting the songs seep through the fingers. I like circling around an idea, especially a new piece. I go looking for a place to enter. The big insight I had into practicing is this: You are practicing alone in order to be with other people. That's how you earn the right. What gives you the right to get on stage and play the songs of those geniuses? Practice.

Anyway, the night in question. I had been having some health issues. I was living with this girl everyone called Mickey. She was a bad seed. I could see it but I didn't want to do anything about it. Just lazy, I guess. She was very impulsive. Came in one day and she's like: I got an abortion because I am not bringing a kid into this ugly world. She was also a wicked drunk who would just trash a place. While I was living with Mickey, I got this disease. No one could name it. I would lose sensation in my fingertips for no reason. The first time it happened I was about to go on stage and it freaked me out. I said something to Walt and he passed around some solos but you could feel the audience getting pissed off. They didn't come here for that. An audience is like a big angry or happy child.

HE'S FULL OF SURPRISES, THAT ONE

NEVER A DAY I DON'T REGRET MY ACTIONS BUT THE WORSE TRUTH, IF I'M BEING TRUTHFUL, IS THAT IF I HAD IT TO DO ALL OVER AGAIN, I WOULD DO EXACTLY THE SAME.

I made an appointment with Doc.

"I can't have it coming over me when I don't expect it."

"There is nothing wrong with you, Dave. You're just old. Why not take it easy?"

"I don't know how to do that. That's like being dead."

"Well, I recommend a psychiatrist."

"No. No talk."

Ash came into the practice space and saw me massaging my hands. I couldn't feel a goddamn thing. He said: You've seen a ghost and that's why you're cold. I felt the rage rising and took my coat, just walked out. I walked for miles. And I'm lazy. I like my apartment; I'm not one to go out. But I felt sure if I went anywhere inside, I would die. Then I come out of this bodega and there's Ash. He said: You're the color of that, and pointed to a fire hydrant. I could see in the window my face was bright red, but my hands were like two chunks of ice. He said: Demons on top of ghosts.

We walked until he said: This is my place. No kidding. Five flights up. It had a nice view but there was nothing in it. I said: You waiting for the moving vans? I put my hand on my chest to check my arrhythmia and my heartbeat was so slow it was like a blues hall grind. Ash's girlfriend came in and we sat on the floor; there weren't any chairs. I took the insurance card out of my wallet and put it on the ground next to me. In case you need that, I tried to say, but it came out like a frog croak. Then Ash took off my coat and my shoes and he stretched me out on the bed, which was just a mattress on the floor. He leaned down close to my ear. He said: I'll bet this day is important; it's an anniversary. My whole body shook.

While I was lying there, Ash's girlfriend took off her clothes.

I'm not kidding. One minute dressed, the next naked as a jay. Then she got into the bed and lay there next to me with all my clothes on. A warm, breathing young girl and a freezing old guy. I felt ashamed because I had no erection. Don't get me wrong, she was beautiful. Her skin was like statue skin. But I had nothing. I wanted to tell Ash that whatever he thought he was

G THERE, ASH'S GIRLFRIEND TOOK

HERE, ASH'S GIRLFRIEND TOOK

E, ASH'S GIRLFRIEND TOOK

SH'S GIRLFRIEND TOOK

OFF HER CLOTHES.

OFF HER CLOTHES.

OFF HER CLOTHES.

OFF HER CLOTHES.

OFF HER CLOTHES.

doing, it was all wrong. But there was no
time because then he took off his clothes and
got next to my other side. If I think about
it, I mean I cannot think about it. I guess
it's just on my mind because here I am, on
my ninetieth birthday, in the last place some
orphaned punk from Plymouth should ever be and
there is an ocean of faces out there, and I
know they have come for me.

He said: She's a blackbelt. You touch her, you
die. And my mind, which might have gone all kind
of places, suddenly remembered this tea set
Granny Lee had. She'd brought it back from the
old country. I used to love to pour water into
the cups, but I was a clumsy kid and I broke one.
I ran off and thought: Now, there's one less, due
to me. It was a memory and then it was like a
dream. I lay in that bed, between those two naked
crazy kids, and the shakes left me. I got up and
walked back to my place. The city lights were
just spectacular. I felt what a knockout Ash's
girl was and I figured I would live.

There's a moment when we're playing. Everyone
is just putting out their notes when for some
reason, I can control but not understand, or
understand but not control, every sound gathers
into a collection that needs all of us. That's
why I was born, to know that. Maybe Ash pulled
that stunt because he was just afraid like we
all are, or simply didn't like losing a paycheck.
But it worked. I'm here and so is he. Curtain
goes up. I step forward. I can kind of feel
the backstage guys around me tense up but I'm
steady. I wave: Welcome; glad you're here.
Glad you're here. **ⓑ**

SHE'S A BLACKBELT.
YOU TOUCH HER, YOU
DIE. AND MY MIND,
WHICH MIGHT HAVE
GONE ALL KIND OF
PLACES, SUDDENLY
REMEMBERED THIS TEA
SET GRANNY LEE HAD.

HONOR ROLL

Nicole Pena

Stephen Spyrit

Nina Simone

Sokhak Peng

Linus Pauling

Jack Ely

Amelia Porterfield

Damian Lillard

Mel Blanc

Emmett Grogan

Melanie Cofield

Matt Fleeger

Monkey, Sandy, Pigsy, Tripitaka

Jack Rawlinson

Sandy Stevenson

Megan Zvezda

Katherine Dunn

CPSIA information can be obtained
at www.ICGtesting.com
Printed in the USA
FSHW01n0337300718
50803FS